MODERN COUPLES?

For my parents

Modern Couples?

Continuity and Change in Heterosexual Relationships

JENNY VAN HOOFF
Manchester Metropolitan University, UK

ASHGATE

Published by
Ashgate Publishing Limited
Wey Court East
Union Road
Farnham
Surrey, GU9 7PT
England

Ashgate Publishing Company
110 Cherry Street
Suite 3-1
Burlington, VT 05401-3818
USA

www.ashgate.com

British Library Cataloguing in Publication Data
Hooff, Jenny van.
    Modern couples? : continuity and change in heterosexual
    relationships.
    1. Man-woman relationships. 2. Couples. 3. Heterosexuals--
    Attitudes.
    I. Title
    306.8'41'08662-dc23

Library of Congress Cataloging-in-Publication Data
van Hooff, Jenny.
    Modern couples? : continuity and change in heterosexual relationships / by Jenny Van Hooff.
        p. cm.
    Includes bibliographical references and index.
    ISBN 978-1-4094-3913-4 (hardback) -- ISBN 978-1-4094-3914-1 (ebook)
1. Couples. 2. Man-woman relationships. 3. Intimacy (Psychology) I. Title.
    HQ801.V279 2012
    306.7--dc23

                                                                          2012030856

ISBN: 9781409439134 (hbk)
ISBN: 9781409439141 (ebk – PDF)
ISBN: 9781409484851 (ebk – ePUB)

Printed and bound in Great Britain by the
MPG Books Group, UK

Contents

Acknowledgements

There are a number of people without whom this book would not have been possible. In particular I am indebted to Penny Tinkler, David Morgan, Jennifer Mason, Lynn Jamieson and colleagues at MMU and LJMU for their encouragement and support. I should also acknowledge the ESRC for funding the research presented here. For their time and willingness to discuss their personal lives with me I am grateful to all of the couples who took part in this study. Finally thanks should go to friends and family for their continuing faith and interest, and most of all to Andrew for just about everything.

Chapter 1
Locating the Couple in Sociological Theory

Intimate relationships, taking the form of family, kin, sexual and couple relationships, along with other associations including friendship, lie at the centre of contemporary sociological debate. Analysis has shifted from rigid conceptualizations of 'the family' as an institution towards the more nuanced category of 'personal life' (Smart, 2007), with an increasing focus on the role that networks of various intimates play in our personal lives (Jamieson et al., 2006). Yet in popular understanding and social reality the couple is often treated as the centre of our intimate and erotic lives (Jamieson, 1998). This book is essentially a qualitative investigation of the expectations and experiences of partners within co-resident heterosexual relationships, which explores the enduring appeal of this type of partnership.

Recent thought about intimacy revolves around the theme of social change, with discussion focusing on the impact of wider societal change on personal relationships. The related processes of individualization, detraditionalization and increased self-reflexivity are generally accepted as the context that has enabled the posited developments in relationships. While the individualization thesis was not at first primarily concerned with intimacy, it has become a core metaphor through which sociological analysis of family life is now pursued (Smart and Shipman, 2004). Within this debate three dominant perspectives have emerged, towards which most of the literature corresponds. These approaches stress either the potential offered by the democratization of intimate relationships, the resulting breakdown of family relationships, or the continuation of traditional inequalities and power structures. The research presented here is essentially an empirical investigation of this ongoing debate, with a particular focus on the changing nature of couple relationships. Before going on to summarize the methodological approach taken, the research is contextualized within wider sociological discussions of intimate relationships.

The Democratization Thesis

The reshaping of personal relationships since the 1960s has led to claims that our intimate lives are the premier site of detraditionalization within late modernity (Gross, 2005: 286). Anthony Giddens is one of the more influential theorists to have written about intimate relationships within the context of a late modern social setting. For this reason the issues raised by his work, in particular the claims made in *The Transformation of Intimacy* (1992) form a major focus of this book. Giddens (1991, 1992) posits the emergence of 'confluent love' and the 'pure relationship' as reflections of a wider social shift towards new forms of self-identity. As the concern here is with the contemporary forms of the late modern heterosexual pair relationship and the changes it has undergone both as an ideology and a social reality in the past few decades, the rhetoric of the pure relationship is particularly relevant in informing my approach.

For Giddens, the emergence of the 'pure relationship' is of key importance for the 'transformation of intimacy', as it is 'prototypical of the new spheres of personal life' (Giddens, 1991: 6). The pure relationship is defined as radically different from traditional forms of personal relationships, as it is internally referential and therefore 'exists solely for whatever rewards that relationship as such can deliver' (Giddens, 1991: 6). Giddens (1992) traces the development of the pure relationship in order to place it in an historical context. He begins with the emergence of 'romantic love', an ideal that was widely diffused in the nineteenth century, when marriage began to lose the economic and kinship ties which were so crucial in premodern arrangements. Pre-industrial marriage was designed to ensure a family's survival as an economic unit and as such was rarely motivated by love (Stone, 1979). With the ensuing separation of the private and public spheres of life, love became celebrated as the main reason for marriage. Middle class couples also began to limit the amount of children they had, and this 'placed a finger on the trigger so far as sexuality was concerned' (Giddens, 1992: 26).

The emphasis placed on love within marriage began a reordering of emotional life and, according to Giddens, introduced the idea of narrative into an individual's life, which refers to the stories by which self-identity is understood both by the individual concerned and others (Giddens, 1992: 39–40). Paradoxically, romantic love was 'essentially feminized love' (Giddens, 1992: 43), although it ensured female subordination by tying women to the home. The extent to which marriage for love came about as a result of industrialization and capitalism, as Giddens maintains, have been questioned, as within Europe free choice of marriage partner predates these developments (Jackson, 1993: 208).

While elements of romantic love ensured the creation of the pure relationship, many of its influences have been destroyed by the emergence of confluent love. The consequences of romantic love for women are incompatible with the egalitarian partnership at the heart of the pure relationship. Confluent love, the successor to romantic love, is an 'active, contingent love' (Giddens, 1992: 61), which 'presumes equality in emotional give and take' (Giddens, 1991: 62). Confluent love differs from romantic love on several points. Firstly, it does not value the 'forever' and 'one and only' (Giddens, 1992: 61) qualities of romantic love, as the finding of a 'special relationship' becomes more important than pledging oneself to a 'special person'. Confluent love also relies on reciprocal sexual pleasure as a core element of a relationship, and in doing so presumes the disappearance of the 'respectable' woman. Furthermore, confluent love is not exclusive to heterosexual relationships, as it is not based on gender difference in the way that romantic love is and it is also not necessarily monogamous. Mutual disclosure is central to confluent love and represents the antithesis of the ideal of mystery, which was so crucial to romantic love. Fragments of romantic love remain, however it is confluent love that characterizes a pure relationship.

Unlike romantic love, confluent love is not anchored to the external conditions of social or economic life, as Giddens maintains earlier ties were, but is free floating, coming to an end whenever it is no longer satisfactory to one or both partners (Giddens, 1992: 58). Trust can no longer be based on exterior factors such as kinship, social duty, or traditional obligation, but, in the context of a pure relationship, 'trust can only be mobilised by a process of mutual disclosure' (Giddens, 1991: 6). As a consequence, a pure relationship is sought only for what it can offer to the partners involved. This is particularly difficult to achieve, as sustaining a relationship that is balanced and rewarding for both partners is one of the 'intrinsic travails' (Giddens, 1991: 91) of a pure relationship. Furthermore, within modern systems of sexual intimacy partners are freely chosen from a plurality of options, of which lonely hearts columns and computer dating are evidence (Giddens, 1991: 87). In this sense late modern intimacy appears to be proactive and is dependent on both partners opening out to the other. Duncombe and Marsden (1993: 10) suggest that increasing expectations of late modern relationships place a premium on the ability to 'do' intimacy rather than just be intimate. This reflects Giddens' view that premodern ties existed out of practicality or birthright, rather than individual desire for fulfilling and intimate relationships.

Reflexivity is also intrinsic to the pure relationship, which depends only on itself, and is therefore necessarily organized around self-examination. Innumerable magazine articles, television programmes, and in particular, self-help manuals, enable continuous monitoring of contemporary personal relationships, and in so doing they operate to 'continuously reconstruct the phenomena they describe' (Giddens, 1991: 92). Within a pure relationship self-identity is developed and affirmed, as it is particularly within intimate relationships that men and women develop a 'narrative of the self' (Giddens, 1992: 75) through mutual disclosure with their partner.

The egalitarian nature of confluent love has consequences not only for personal relationships, but also for wider society. To quote, 'a symmetry exists between the democratising of personal life and democratic possibilities in the global political order at the most extensive level' (Giddens, 1992: 195–6). Giddens locates the emergence of the pure relationship, not only in couple relationships, but also in parent-child relations and other forms of kinship and friendship. Confluent love will therefore bring an end to differential power in social life as individuals have to reflexively examine and justify their own conduct (Giddens, 1992: 193).

If accurate, the developments described by Giddens will have had a profound influence on the types of relationships that individuals seek out and form. Not only are such relationships based on mutual disclosure and democracy, but they must also include an exploration of each partner's sexual preferences, which are now divorced from heteronormativity. While he is vague about the timing of these developments, it would appear that they are related to the 'sexual revolution' and therefore can be pinned down to the 'past several decades' (Giddens, 1992: 1). Although his initial claims were made in the early 1990s, Giddens remains arguably the most prominent and influential commentator to have contributed to the debate (Gillies, 2003) and the research presented here is largely an empirical investigation of the suggested transformation of intimacy.

Giddens is by no means the only theorist to claim that sweeping changes have revolutionized personal life in the West. While Francesca Cancian's (1987) work is located in late 1980s North America at the height of the Reagan/Bush era, it predates Giddens' account as a defence of the process of individualization on family life. Her work was in part a response to the pessimistic assertions of scholars such as Christopher Lasch (1979) and Robert Bellah (1985) that intimate relations have been strained to breaking point by the individualism of recent decades.

Cancian argues the case for a late modern image of intimacy that 'combines enduring love with self-development' (Cancian, 1987: 3). She examines three popular images of heterosexual relationships; firstly the 'traditional marriage', which the right wing regards as central to maintaining family relationships and which is based on inegalitarian gender roles. This type of relationship holds the wife responsible for intimacy and other emotional labour, and Cancian argues that it will persist as an important blueprint for close relationships as long as the division of labour remains stable (Cancian, 1987: 50). The second type of relationship, termed the 'independence relationship', emerged in the 1960s, and regards love as the equal responsibility of both partners, and emphasizes the self to the point of avoiding obligations. Cancian believes that a third type of intimacy, which she terms the 'interdependence' blueprint, successfully reconciles the commitment valued by the traditional marriage, and the self-development crucial to the Independence blueprint. Within the interdependence relationship, love is androgynous, rather than particularly feminine, and is concerned with the quality of the relationship, rather than fulfilling traditional marital duties. The shift towards more androgynous definitions of love is mirrored by androgynous conceptions of the ideal self, as a developed person is defined as someone who combines feminine intimacy and emotional expression with masculine independence and competence (Cancian, 1987: 8).

Cancian traces the different 'family blueprints' that have dominated the social organization of marriage (Cancian, 1987: 31) since the transition from agrarian to capitalist society polarized gender roles and feminized love. The dominant Western nineteenth-century ideal is that of 'family duty', which tied love to women's family duties. This was succeeded by the 'companionship' blueprint, which encouraged intimacy within marriage, and is similar in definition to romantic love, as it is dependent on the separation of home and work, with love regarded as a feminine task because marriage remained more the centre of the wife's life. Like Giddens' (1992) transformation of intimacy, Cancian also dates the shift towards androgynous love from the mid-1960s.

The interdependence blueprint for intimacy prefigures Giddens' pure relationship, as it also emphasizes the importance of self-development within committed personal relationships, and the gender equality that necessarily precedes this; Cancian's point that since the 1970s, 'intimate relationships in the private sphere became the main arena for developing one's unique self' (Cancian, 1987: 27) has parallels with Giddens' work. Similarly, the interdependent relationship is seen as central to self-development, as, using object-relations theory, Cancian argues that selves develop out of past relationships and are maintained by present relationships, in the same way that secure relationships in childhood enable children to develop from total dependency to interdependence (Cancian, 1987: 114). Unlike Giddens, Cancian argues that interdependent love cannot be achieved solely through mutual disclosure, but also through physical activity, care and productive work, which she regards as some of the most important human capacities (Cancian, 1987: 121). She acknowledges several potential problems with the interdependent relationship, including an over-emphasis on self-disclosure at the expense of material interdependence which may cause people to withdraw from public life into the safety of their personal relationships (Cancian, 1987: 9). However, she maintains that it is a preferable style of intimacy than the sex-stereotyped traditional relationship, or the shallow independent relationship.

A recurring theme in Giddens' work is female equality as a necessary precondition for the pure relationship to exist, and he proclaims 'today, for the first time in history, women claim equality with men' (Giddens, 1992: 1). Women have largely pioneered the transformation of intimacy, and as male sexual control over women has been broken down, new emotional antagonisms are opening up between the sexes (Giddens, 1992: 153). Male claims to power on the basis of their gender are now obsolete; consequently men are torn between 'assertive sexual dominance, including the use of violence, on the one hand, and constant anxieties about potency on the other' (Giddens, 1992: 118). Giddens concedes that gender equality is not yet fully established in all areas of life;

however, he maintains that within personal relationships, 'utopianism here can be readily offset by realism' (Giddens, 1992: 180). Same-sex, especially lesbian, relationships were the first to achieve the pure relationship status because of their high rates of dissolution as well as their high levels of communication, prompting Giddens to claim 'it is the gays who are the pioneers' (Giddens, 1992: 135). However, Giddens argues that at this point confluent love is no longer limited to same-sex relationships, as 'reasonably durable sexual ties, marriages and friendship relations all tend to approximate today to the pure relationship' (Giddens, 1991: 87). It would seem unlikely that marriage qualifies as a pure, dyadic, detraditionalized relationship, as external approval has obviously been sought. However, Giddens is insistent that 'marriage becomes more and more a relationship initiated for, and kept going as long as it delivers emotional satisfaction to be delivered for close contact with another' (Giddens, 1991: 89). This analysis is based on the high rates of divorce and remarriage apparent in Western Europe. Similarly, Beck and Beck-Gernsheim (1995, 2002) have stressed the role of individualization in releasing men and women from gender roles. While they acknowledge that men have not yet clarified their position, they insist that traditional ideas about gender have lost their hold.

More recent accounts of intimacy have also suggested that modern social processes enable individuals to engage in more rewarding intimate relationships. The features of Giddens' late modernity correlate in many ways with those of Beck's 'risk society' (1992) in which awareness of risk forms the axis of social organization. Risk society is accompanied by 'reflexive modernisation' (Beck, 1994) through which industrial society confronts its own limits and consequences (Adkins, 2001). Beck (1992) considers two aspects of reflexive modernization; firstly the shift from a preoccupation with wealth production to the focus on risk production. Evidence of this is the recent media preoccupation with health or environmental risks, for example foot and mouth disease, BSE and climate change, as opposed to an earlier focus on the achievements of capitalism. The second aspect of reflexive modernization is concerned with the self and the constant monitoring of our own actions. As the certainties of modern society dissolve, the solutions offered lack any well-founded basis. Therefore the result of reflexive modernization is increased individualization, whereby biography, which was once restricted by traditional guidelines, becomes 'elective' (Beck and Beck-Gernsheim, 1995: 25). While the nineteenth century was the century of 'either/or', reflecting a suspicion of ambiguity, the late twentieth century is characterized by 'and', which suggests the possibility of alternative explanations or methods (Beck, 1997, cited in Morgan, 1999: 24). The aforementioned element of risk is also on a personal level, as success is not guaranteed and cannot be planned in the long-term, as the 'do-it-yourself biography can become the breakdown biography' (Beck and Beck-Gernsheim, 2002: 6), hence the fragility of intimate relationships.

Beck and Beck-Gernsheim (1995, 2002) maintain that the traditional nuclear family is falling apart on issues such as emancipation and equal rights, which they interpret as a positive development, as in the place of the obsolete traditional family negotiated, alternative families are emerging. Here the key term is individualization, resulting in an end to the fixed meanings of words such as 'love', 'sexuality', and 'marriage', which now mean something different to each individual (Beck and Beck-Gernsheim, 1995: 4, 5). What used to be undertaken as a matter of course by heterosexual couples, for example getting married and having children, now has to be discussed, negotiated and justified, as individuals are compelled to problematize their decisions and actions. However, Beck and Beck-Gernsheim have no doubts that within our impersonal and uncertain societies the meaning of life is 'love, our secular religion' (Beck and Beck-Gernsheim, 1995: 168). They maintain that as industrial society collapses along with its fixed gender and occupational roles, individuals are forced to search for personal satisfaction, and that love has become the new centre around which our detraditionalized lives revolve, and has 'become a blank that the lovers must fill in themselves' (Beck and Beck-Gernsheim, 1995: 5). There is an acknowledgement that individualization is not an entirely new phenomenon, however, for Beck and Beck-Gernsheim what is revolutionary is the mass character of individualization which they posit as exclusive to modern Western societies.

Beck and Beck-Gernsheim portray late modern couple relationships as detraditionalized and based on the principles of personal freedom and satisfaction, thereby supporting Giddens' claims. Unlike Giddens, however, they argue that the changes in personal relationships have come about because of the unique character of contemporary individualization. They are also less optimistic about the possibilities that these changes have resulted in and acknowledge that they can generate anxiety and uncertainty.

The detraditionalization approach stresses the importance of continuous monitoring of relationships and notes in particular the role that self-help and therapy has to play in this. For Giddens, self-help manuals are 'texts of our time' (Giddens, 1992: 64), and their proliferation is interpreted as evidence for the existence of the pure relationship, as they are 'expressions of the reflexivity which they chart out and help shape' (Giddens, 1992: 64). Beck and Beck-Gernsheim also understand the late modern market for self-help as evidence for a profound change in personal life, as individuals lack communal guidelines and search for something else to provide answers and instructions. Both Beck and Beck-Gernsheim and Giddens posit rising divorce rates as further evidence for their arguments. Weeks (1995) also interprets the decline in marriage as a sign of a fundamental shift within heterosexual relationships toward a democratic ideal based upon negotiation and equality, with women in particular willing to leave an unsatisfactory relationship. He argues that late modern social processes have radically transformed sexualities and personal relationships. Weeks acknowledges that the changes in intimate relationships coexist with a number of deeply sedimented traditions, yet despite the persistence of traditional ideals, Weeks insists that within intimate relationships there is a move towards equality. He stresses the way in which sexuality and sexual behaviour are now based on choice, as opposed to being socially proscribed. Similarly, Plummer (1995) argues that the many discourses of intimacy circulating in the late modern world offer the potential for new forms of emancipation. He uses the concept 'intimate citizenship' to describe how political claims have been made through the articulation of personal and sexual narratives, and emphasizes the importance of intimate relations at the beginning of the twenty-first century.

The possible consequences of late modernity bring moral questions into prominence. Beck and Beck-Gernsheim concede that the increased demands on individuals may result in them failing to consider the consequences or morality of their actions. However, despite the risks, they dispute the argument that individualization will eradicate social cohesion (Beck and Beck-Gernsheim, 2002). Giddens acknowledges the problem of moral uncertainty within late modern society, which can be illustrated in environmental issues, the ethical issues bound up in reproduction technology, the effects of globalization and, most importantly for our purposes, the morality bound up in the project of the self, which is guided only by a 'morality of authenticity' (Giddens, 1991: 225). Giddens believes that the 'possibility of intimacy means the promise of democracy' (1992: 187), envisaging the development of an ethical framework, founded upon principles of trust, accountability and democracy. Weeks (1995) also expresses concern with the consequences of growing individualization on morality. However, writing from a standpoint of what he terms 'radical humanism', he proposes an ethic of love founded on four principles; care, responsibility, respect and knowledge. Overall, Weeks, like Giddens, is optimistic about the future of personal relationships.

Late modern relationships are portrayed as negotiated and democratized by the authors of reflexive change, as detailed in this section. The changes posited here are of such magnitude that their influence should, in theory, have radically changed individuals' expectations and experiences of intimate relationships. However, this approach lacks sufficient empirical evidence. Before considering the findings of existing research on family and couple relationships I discuss pessimistic interpretations of the developments posited here.

The Breakdown of Intimate Relationships

However close we are to achieving confluent or androgynous love in our personal lives, we have to question whether the proposed changes in intimacy are beneficial or harmful. In contrast with the optimism Giddens, Cancian and, to a lesser extent, Beck and Beck-Gernsheim display about the future of intimate relationships, other theorists have raised concerns about the consequences of modern life upon intimacy, often in work predating the more optimistic texts. For example, in his influential book, *The Triumph of the Therapeutic*, Philip Reiff (1966) argued that cultural controls, based on obedience and faith, save us from chaos and emptiness. However, the therapeutic world, which he observed the development of in the 1960s, is anti-culture and substitutes individual feelings and desires for faith in a collective morality.

In 1979 Christopher Lasch published his reflections on the 'me decade' in *The Culture of Narcissism*; many of his observations are as applicable in the early twenty-first century as they were in the 1970s. He proposed that the pursuit of happiness has led to the dead end of narcissistic preoccupation with the self as a result of the anxieties and uncertainties of modern life. The ideal of true romance places an impossible burden upon most relationships, as we demand too much from life and not enough from ourselves, consequently 'personal relations crumble under the emotional weight with which they are burdened' (Lasch, 1979: 188). By extending individualism into the family, capitalism deliberately undermines the ability of the family to resist the lure of instant gratification. The war of the sexes, Lasch notes, is set to intensify as women are encouraged to hate men and are exposed to repeated disappointments while in turn men attempt to reassert their dominance through acts of violence. The image presented by Lasch is a far cry from the harmonious and egalitarian pure relationship. He has inevitably received criticism from feminists who regard his work as an attack on sensitive mothering, which he saw as destroying patriarchal authority (Jamieson, 1998: 48). However, this should not detract from his observation of the anxiety felt by men and women as they attempt to find some meaning in what he regarded as a world devoid of human values. Slater argues that the type of self-obsession encouraged by excessive consumption is further evidence of narcissism (Slater, 1997: 92). Far from referring to self-love, Slater defines narcissism as resulting from an inadequate sense of self, which is further exploited by consumer culture.

Richard Sennet (1977) was also critical of the decline of traditional regulations for personal relationships. For him conversation has taken on the form of confession, as people have come to believe that public activity should reveal inner personality. As the boundaries between the individual and the rest of the world collapse, social cohesion is damaged and desire becomes the guiding principle of modern life. Jamieson (1998) notes the difficulty in reaching firm conclusions on the consequences of late modernity. Certain events, for example the trends in cohabitation, divorce and remarriage, are used as evidence by both sides in the debate. Cancian believes that criticism of the trend from role to self stems from a belief that people need constraining rules and strong community ties (Cancian, 1987: 57). While agreeing with Cancian that this argument is anti-democratic, I would argue that more recent critiques of late modern social trends (Adkins, 1999; Slater, 1997) are valid in that they question the way that reflexivity is ordered in terms of gender and class, and recognize the problems that are inherent in a society when individuals are consumers rather than citizens.

Cancian critiques the pessimistic approach using the perspectives of classical sociological theories (Cancian, 1987: 51–64). She argues that the central issue is one of constraint versus freedom; do people need greater freedom or stronger social controls to provide security and structure? Proponents of the functionalist perspective, including Durkheim and Parsons, would argue that social rules are needed in order to limit desires and define a meaningful way of life which binds individuals together in a secure and moral community. Durkheim believed that without proper social integration we become excessively self-centred, despairing, and possibly suicidal. Ferdinand Tönnies was also sceptical of the shift towards 'gesellschaft', or society, characterized by impersonal, superficial relationships, from the kinship and community ties of 'gemeinschaft'. I would agree with Cancian's argument that past relationships were not always warm and secure. Gillis (1996) has shown how our nostalgia for 'traditional' relationships leads us to ignore the problems experienced in pre-modern family life, as, for example, short life expectancy resulted in as many families being broken up by death as are broken by divorce today.

Zygmunt Bauman has established himself as a vocal detractor of the individualization process, which he describes in near-apocalyptic terms. He argues that the uncertainty which pervades modern society works to divide individuals and undermines the 'common interest' (Bauman, 2000: 148). He writes that in attempting to release individuals from their inherited identity and encourage a shift from ascription to achievement, contemporary society has failed to provide a stable backdrop in which individuals can 'cast their anchor' (Bauman, 1995: 204). Consequently, the post-modern condition of uncertainty is permanent and irreducible, as we lack sufficient resources with which to build a secure identity, while our fears and anxieties are suffered alone. Bauman argues that the plurality of choices on offer to us are not necessarily a positive phenomenon, as 'if you may never err, you can never be sure of being in the right either. If there are no wrong moves, there is nothing to distinguish a move from a better one' (Bauman, 2000: 63). The freedoms offered within late modernity have ensured that while there are no wrongs, there are no rights either, thus compounding this condition of uncertainty. The advent of a free-floating capitalism is replicated in the trend from marriage to cohabitation, which for Bauman includes the assumption that the relationship may be broken at any minute, for any reason, once the need or desire has dried up (Bauman, 2000: 149). While staying together is a matter of reciprocal agreement, disengagement is unilateral thus undermining the equality necessary in late modern relationships. From this perspective human bonds and partnerships are treated as things to be consumed rather than worked on and produced and as such are subjected to the same criteria of evaluation as consumer goods (Bauman, 2000: 163), which can be illustrated by the modern dependency on experts for self-direction.

Bauman goes on to argue that the consequences of post modernity vary according to class and ethnicity. Where people are trapped in poverty and deprivation, frustration and fear materialize in violence which is often directed towards the stranger; 'if the contented and secure wax lyrical about the beauty of nationhood ... the insecure and hounded bewail the defilement and humiliation of their race' (Bauman, 1995: 212). Personal relationships are the preferred, and possibly only way of community building, however their intrinsic fragility means that they are unable to resist this pressure (Bauman, 2000: 50). It would appear that the rights of individuals are as polarized as they ever were, a point Giddens ignores; he claims that modernity produces difference, exclusion and marginalization, but that lifestyle choices can still be made under severe material constraint (Giddens, 1991: 6). Bauman (2000) argues that plastic sexuality and the pure relationship reflect aspects of the commodification of human partnerships. While Giddens interprets them as elements of the autonomy offered to us within late modern society, Bauman believes that this only applies to the 'rich and mighty' (Bauman, 2000: 89), if at all; 'one can support Giddens' assertion whole-heartedly only if one focuses on the stronger and more resourceful members of partnerships, which necessarily include also the weaker, not so lavishly endowed with the resources needed to freely follow their desires' (ibid).

Bauman also describes the way in which social skills are undermined by excessive concern with individualism and consumerism, as, unable to cope, we turn to 'marketable goods, services or expert council' (Bauman, 1987: 164). The ambivalence of modern life is all-pervasive; within personal relationships it is no longer clear what the norm is. The ubiquitous fear of either being accused of, or suffering from, abuse and harassment contradicts the manner in which post-modern society eulogizes the delights of sex; 'all pursuit of happiness is ... shot through with fear' (Bauman, 1998: 32). Personal relations are seen as frail, amoral and superficial; even friendship is seen to be motivated by self-interest. Bauman's view stands in stark contrast to Giddens' description of late modern intimacy, as he is also sceptical of self-reflexivity, seeing constant monitoring of the self as stemming from the self-obsessed consumerism that threatens to destroy personal relationships. With satisfaction as the driving force in relationships, the necessary compromise involved in commitment is rendered impossible.

Proponents of the pessimistic approach portray the increased significance of intimacy as a symptom of the self-obsessed nature of consumer culture. Positive values of love, care and responsibility are presented as unsustainable in a culture promoting choice and personal freedom at the expense of long term commitments to family and parenting (Gillies, 2003: 11). Parallels in the fears of pessimistic authors with New Right thinkers who predict the collapse of the family and moral standards have been noted (Gillies, 2003). However, Bauman and Lasch can be defended from this accusation, as they are not motivated by right wing concerns, but by the alienation felt by many sections of society. The feminist author Fay Weldon has also critiqued the cult of therapism in her 1993 novel *Affliction* and it could not be argued that she was motivated by the New Right agenda. Similarly, Mary Evans (2003) has written critically of the commercialization of love from a feminist perspective. Cancian accuses detractors of the changes in personal relationships of romanticizing the past. While this may be true of the reactionary right, the reservations that the above theorists have of a world dominated by market values are valid. Although any change that breaks down inequalities of all kinds can only be positive, there is little substantial evidence to suggest that class and gender relations are no longer polarized.

The authors detailed above uncritically accept the claim that personal relationships have been detraditionalized, although their interpretations of the impact of this differ. A body of work seeking to interrogate this premise has emerged as a reaction to these claims.

Continuity

Although the contrasting positions detailed so far dominate contemporary understanding of family and personal relationships, a third perspective has emerged which questions the extent to which intimate relationships have been transformed. For theorists who reject claims of both breakdown and democratization, the presumed changes in personal relationships are profoundly overstated (Gillies, 2003: 16). Gillies highlights the danger of interpreting the past and predicting the future through rigid, theoretically tinted lenses, and questions the empirical basis of such claims. In this section critiques of the dominant positions are discussed.

While Giddens maintains that reflexive modernization has resulted in the dissolution of structural inequalities based on class, gender and race, Scott Lash (1994) argues that reflexivity depends upon access to information and communication structures which particularly exclude women. He uses the example of a single mother living in an urban ghetto who possesses little reflexivity because she is constrained by structural poverty (Lash, 1994: 120). Lash identifies two forms of reflexivity; firstly 'structural reflexivity', in which agency is released from structure, and is then compelled to reflect on the rules and resources of such a structure, something that is illustrated by Beck's ecological critique in the context of risk society. The second form of reflexivity identified by Lash is 'self-reflexivity', through which individuals reflect on themselves, resulting in Giddens' 'narrative of the self'. The latter is particularly important in the discussion of late modern relationship forms, and presupposes an element of detraditionalization and individualization. Developing this analysis, Adkins (1999) argues that gender is neither straightforwardly broken down nor reproduced by reflexive modernization, rather new configurations of gender are produced. While critics have cast doubt on the universality of reflexive modernization as a social shift, an exploration of the extent to which reflexivity is characteristic of late modern relationships is also necessary, and will form a theme of my research.

The emergence of a 'post-traditional' society, whereby everyday life has become detraditionalized, underpins the analysis of the proponents of social change. The impact of mass media and modern communications has resulted in traditions being lifted out of local contexts of interaction and losing their relevance. Consequently, the options and uncertainties of modern culture on both local and global levels supersede the security and parochialism of traditional life. Reflexivity is understood to have replaced tradition as a way of organizing personal life, as people are forced to make lifestyle choices, rather than fall in to roles expected of them. Appeals to traditional symbols and practices are in themselves reflexively organized and therefore are not opposed to internally referential social systems, but are instead part of them (Giddens, 1991: 150), as they are argued to have been reflexively chosen from a number of alternatives including non-traditional options.

It is apparent that a degree of detraditionalization is taking place, however, as Paul Heelas (1996) maintains, this does not automatically mean that we are launching into a post-traditional age. Heelas uses the worldwide resurgence of nationalism and ethnic conflict to illustrate the point that the individual is not ruling our times. Detraditionalization is taking place alongside tradition-maintenance, retraditionalization and the construction of new traditions (Heelas, 1996: 2). The result is a society where the individual may have to lead a contradictory life, caught between the traditional demands of public life and the detraditionalized freedom of private life (Heelas, 1996: 10). Furthermore, drawing on the work of Bellah, Heelas indicates that the very faith in the value of individualism may be tradition informed. The suggestion that we have had a radical break with the past may oversimplify modern social processes. It could be argued that the view of modern and premodern societies simply as 'traditional' ignores the complex interplay between structure and agency and risks oversimplifying historical change. The premise that traditions were pregiven structures has also been critiqued, as they have always been open to human agency (Luke, 1996).

The detraditionalization thesis has been further critiqued by Gross (2005) as providing an inadequate account of social change. He distinguishes between two different types of tradition, firstly 'regulative traditions' (Gross, 2005: 293), which are essentially external in nature, with transgressions punished by exclusion from various moral communities. While the changes in personal relationships over the past few decades represent an undeniable decline in regulative traditions, 'meaning-constitutive traditions' (2005: 295), or the ideals and practices passed down from previous generations, persist and have come to be accepted as normative. Intimate relationships remain organized around the heteronormative hegemonic ideal, on the basis of ideas and practices that are handed down from the past 'that may assume a naturalized and taken-for-granted form, free though agents may be from external constraints that would force them to adopt those ideas and practices' (2005: 306).

Giddens' reliance on self-help texts and manuals as the grounding for his research has also been challenged (Shumway, 2003; Jamieson, 1999). Drawing on Foucault, he reiterates his assertion that 'discourse becomes constitutive of the social reality it portrays' (Giddens, 1992: 28). In this way concepts promoted in all areas of life, for example, sociological theory and therapeutic discourse seep back in to social life and help to shape what they seek to explain. However, Giddens explicitly rejects Foucault's description of this as a way of controlling and regulating social organization, and instead portrays it as a two-way 'institutional reflexivity' (Giddens, 1992: 28). For Foucault, the rise of therapy and counselling is a way of 'regulating procedures for the confession of sex' (cited in Giddens, 1992: 30). Giddens maintains that this view is 'simply mistaken', as self-help and therapy represents increasing autonomy and reflexivity. A review of the themes of several best-selling relationship manuals (van Hooff, 2001) revealed the favouring of a white, heterosexual norm within these texts. The manuals were also explicitly targeted towards a female readership, and placed the burden of emotional labour of maintaining the relationship upon the female partner's shoulders. This runs counter to the pure relationship in which emotions are dealt with in a reciprocal manner. Rather than representing a final break with tradition, to a large extent these texts promoted a continuation of traditional gender roles, and in doing so contributed to a process of tradition maintenance within personal relationships. In this way, self-help manuals can be seen as agents of social control, rather than reflecting increasing individual autonomy. Jamieson notes that Giddens 'draws relatively uncritically on therapeutic literature, as documents about and symptoms of personal and social change' (Jamieson, 1999: 480). It has also been noted that the majority of self-help guides are concerned with heterosexual marriage, rather than detraditionalized forms of intimacy (Shumway, 2003).

Hawkes (1996) reviewed a number of 'lifestyle journals' to find that the tone of the majority of articles in *Cosmopolitan* and other women's magazines continued to prioritize male sexual experience, as 'a sense of autonomy of self, particularly for women, is negated in the exhortations to stoke the fires of desire' (Hawkes, 1996: 119). Sex has become the central dynamic of the late modern pair relationship, and 'in this brave new age of sex, the greatest sin is sexual boredom' (Hawkes, 1996: 119). For Hawkes, this does not reflect increasing autonomy and individual freedom, but maintains key hegemonic ideals, as the parameters of sexual and erotic success are derived from those of heterosexual coitus. In this way it is argued that 'good housekeeping has now been replaced by 'good sex-making'' (Hawkes, 1996: 121) as a late modern feminine ideal. Hawkes concludes that although sex has been largely uncoupled from monogamy and reproduction it retains a deep-seated connection with patriarchal sexual relations.

A more critical interpretation of the role of self-help would suggest that it symbolizes the way in which society has come to dominate the individual through consumer goods, which are now not only necessary for survival, but are also required in the construction of self-identity. What Giddens celebrates as freedom from traditional constraints is interpreted by Slater (1997: 83) as the loss of natural feeling and stable social values, which has resulted in the disorientation and subjugation of the individual. Slater explains that consumerism simultaneously exploits the mass identity crisis apparent within modern society by promoting goods as the solutions to problems of identity, and in the process intensifies it by offering 'ever more plural values and ways of being' (Slater, 1997: 88). Slater goes on to describe late modernity as an expert culture, in which individuals rely on self-help manuals, magazines and television programmes for guidance. As the social is reduced to the level of the individual, people turn to therapeutic works in their search for meaning and authenticity. However, according to Slater, 'it is a cure which renders the disease even more chronic' (1997: 97). Furedi (2003) argues that something more sinister is at work in his critique of therapeutic culture, proposing that the therapeutic ethos is primarily about imposing a new conformity through the management of people's emotions. In sum, the idea that reliance on therapy and self-help guides is a positive development indicative of greater freedom is problematic at best.

It could be argued that Giddens has largely failed to distinguish between the pure relationship as ideology and practice. David Morgan (1991) notes that 'ideology' is one of the most troublesome concepts in sociology, and he addresses a number of problems in its general use. Morgan stresses the difficulty in defining ideology, as it is hard to say what a 'non-ideological statement' is (Morgan, 1991: 115). He also writes that in regard to marriage and the family, there exists not one unified ideology, but a plurality, and that there may be an overlapping of ideologies specifically concerned with the family. The influence of a particular ideology is also difficult to measure, as even where individuals do conform to mainstream ideologies, this may be because of a lack of viable alternatives. Morgan argues that certain ideological constructions of marriage, for example the assumed twentieth-century change from institution to relationship, can be identified with particular sets of professionals concerned with marriage and marital problems, including therapists and the authors of therapeutic manuals. However, describing marriage as a relationship in this way has the adverse effect of obscuring gender inequalities rather than undermining them.

While Morgan (1991: 135) rejects the 'hypodermic' model, in which ideology is seen as being directly influential on the actions of individuals, he acknowledges that various ideologies do impact on everyday practices. Jamieson (1998: 158) argues that 'practices, private stories and public stories are not neatly separate, but interconnected and mutually creating', however, she proposes that the shift towards the pure relationship and its emphasis on disclosing intimacy is 'too selective a story to be anything other than a very partial picture of an emerging future' (1998: 159). Jamieson suggests that public stories have changed more dramatically than private practices, and although people draw on public stories to make sense of their own lives, the two do not provide neat reflections of each other (1998: 158).

Nicklass Luhmann (1986) has described how forms of intimacy evolve through contemporary literature, as novels, plays, and more recently self-help manuals, provide a link between intimacy as a social system and a personal experience. Giddens draws on this, yet he acknowledges that the ideals portrayed in nineteenth century romantic novels were not attained within romantic love, which usually resulted in 'grim, domestic subjection' (Giddens, 1992: 62). However, he presents little evidence to suggest that the pure relationship could have different consequences and also fails to consider that the lived experiences of confluent love could be any different from the relationship ideals promoted in manuals and magazines.

Jamieson (1999) notes that the idea that personal life has become more intimate and individualized than ever before is not a new concept. She indicates that Scottish Enlightenment philosophers saw intimacy as emerging in their time. Jamieson also describes the way that three decades before *The Transformation of Intimacy*, Berger and Kellner (1964) noted that the private sphere was being released from public controls, and yet was defined and utilized as the main social arena for individual's self-realization. Berger and Kellner start with the even earlier insight of Durkheim that marriage serves as a protection against anomie, thus helping individuals achieve a sense of stability. The pure relationship also has echoes of Young and Willmott's (1975) heavily critiqued 'symmetrical family', in which conjugal roles, although not interchangeable, are similar in terms of the emotional and practical contributions made by each spouse. Giddens' description of the pure relationship as 'explosive' (1992: 2) is then perhaps a little premature. Similarly, Gillies (2003) argues that it is ethnocentric to portray individualism as a newly emerging characteristic. She cites Goldbourne and Chamberlain's (1998) study, which notes that within African-Caribbean family and community relations, choice and negotiation are well established principles.

Jamieson writes a compelling critique of the idea of the family as the site of equality and democracy. Empirical evidence suggests that gender inequalities remain, for example when choosing whether or not to opt out of domestic work and childcare, men exercise considerably more power than women (Jamieson, 1999: 484). This would indicate that even when heterosexual couples do make non-sexist living arrangements, it is ultimately the decision of the male partner as women do not have the same freedom of choice. Yet it would appear that persistent gender inequalities do not prevent many couples from forming intimate and caring relationships, a point which contradicts the view that true intimacy is only possible within a context of the pure relationship. Research indicates that creative energy is deployed in disguising inequality, rather than undermining it (Bittman and Lovejoy, cited in Jamieson, 1999: 485). In doing this, many couples admit that their domestic labour is organized along traditionally gendered lines, yet claim that this is only temporary and is based on practical reasons. Here we return to the influence of public discourse over private life; ideology is influential, but does not always extend so far as to radically alter practical decisions.

Giddens maintains that a radical transformation of intimacy is under way, with profound consequences for men and women, both in personal relationships and wider society. Unfortunately his account is flawed on various levels. The self-reflexivity that he and Beck and Beck-Gernsheim present as characteristic of late modernity appears to be distributed on a hierarchical scale, according to gender. Giddens proceeds to oversimplify gender issues in his conclusion that men and women are heading for greater equality, and in doing so glosses over feminist arguments. He interprets the rise in popularity of self-help as indicative of the emergence of the pure relationship, however a brief review of a selection of such manuals suggests otherwise. Evidence has failed to support an optimistic account of the democratization of personal life; empirical evidence of the pure relationship has yet to be produced. Although some of the pessimistic accounts, such as those of Lasch and Sennet, may go too far in their predictions for the end of meaningful relationships, their claims are based upon the same evidence as Giddens' argument. In claiming openness as a constructive social process, Giddens bases part of his analysis on 'a rather unpacked psychological theory' (Jamieson, 1999: 481). Jamieson refers to Simmel's warning against the mutual disclosure that Giddens celebrates, as he claimed that a total lack of secrets could destroy a relationship.

It cannot be denied that modern life is evolving rapidly as older institutions lose their meaning. Detraditionalization is not necessarily the inevitable outcome, however, as it is accompanied by processes of tradition maintenance. In the face of public ideals to the contrary, gender inequalities within personal relationships may be included in areas of retraditionalization and tradition maintenance. In his defence, Giddens concedes that his work is analytical rather than descriptive (1991: 2). It is perhaps a little early to conclude on the consequences of a social process that has only recently started; the purpose of this study is to explore the above debate and to further our understanding of late-modern heterosexual relationships in Britain, rather than to conclusively prove the existence or otherwise of the pure relationship.

Although Cancian used detailed research findings to illustrate her argument that interdependent love was a prominent ideal in 1980s America, Giddens does not qualify his theories of late modern intimacy with any empirical evidence. However it is possible to use other studies, for example those focussing on the gendered division of domestic labour, to analyse whether the equality that is intrinsic to the pure relationship is apparent in heterosexual couple's everyday practices. Jamieson (1998, 1999) has reviewed recent research for signs of change predicted in Giddens' optimistic account, to find that the majority of research in this field is concerned with the perceived change from the traditional relationship, with a strict gendered division of labour, to an egalitarian partnership. As increasing numbers of women take up formal employment, a corresponding rise in male participation in domestic labour has been assumed. However, research over the past two decades suggests that inequalities remain; 'heterosexual coupledom remains surprisingly organized around man-as-the-main-earner and woman-as-domestic-worker/carer despite the prevalence of dual earner households' (Jamieson, 1998: 138). Jamieson cites a number of studies (Rosen, 1987; Nickols and Metzen, 1982; Pahl, 1984) that document a rise in men's participation in domestic labour where their wives are working. However, in these cases the extra work done by husbands was comparatively insignificant, compared to the extra work taken on by women, leading to the suggestion that women endure a double burden of housework and paid employment.

Jane Lewis (2001) challenges the individualism thesis through her qualitative research of a generation of older married couples and a younger generation of married and cohabiting couples with dependent children. The shift from marriage to cohabitation has been used as evidence of rising individualism by both optimistic (Beck and Beck-Gernsheim, 1995, 2002) and pessimistic (Bauman, 1995, 2000) camps. While Lewis found that her younger respondents enjoyed greater reflexivity in comparison to their parent's generation, she concluded that there was no evidence to suggest that a greater concern with self-development had undermined commitment within relationships (Lewis, 2001: 180). Lewis also found little evidence to support the idea of gender equality, either within paid or unpaid work, although this was at least something that was up for discussion for the younger generation. Lewis' research led her to conclude that while self-interest may motivate individuals, this does not come at the expense of commitment within relationships.

An earlier study of British marriage (Gillis, 1985) revealed that the popular ideology of equality dissolved in marriage, as when couples become homeowners and parents their relationship becomes overwhelmed with stereotyped roles. Gillis notes that this was the cause of many marital problems, as when the conjugal ideal is confronted with reality, particularly with the birth of the first child, marital breakdown may follow. In one sense, Gillis's findings could be seen as indicative of the pure relationship, as in many cases couples refuse to remain in an unequal partnership. However, Gillis argues that as women are usually given the task of childcare, their only option is remarriage, thus sparking a cycle of dependency in which late modern ideals are not reflected.

Judith Stacey (1996) conducted three years of fieldwork on families in Silicon Valley in California during the 1980s. As a consequence, her work centres on the debate over family values, which peaked in America at this time. However, her findings are also relevant to this study, as she was interested in the extent to which her respondents' lives were mirrored by Shorter's definition of the 'postmodern family' (cited in Stacey, 1996: 7), which refers to three trends of Western family life; firstly, the decline of parental influence over the young in favour of peer influence; secondly, widespread marital instability, and finally, women's departure from the nest. Stacey found that white, middle class families were the propagandists and principal beneficiaries of contemporary family changes, as they represented the minority who had the kinds of resources that enabled them to realize the potential of postmodern family options. In most households, Stacey's research indicated that the multiple earner strategy was more a response to financial pressure than it was to feminism. However, Stacey argues that working class women had been more successful than some feminist research shows, 'although the division of household labour remains profoundly inequitable, a major gender norm has shifted here' (Stacey, 1996: 27). Stacey's findings do provide a limited amount of evidence in support of the claims of theorists such as Giddens (1991, 1992) and Beck and Beck-Gernsheim (1995, 2002). However, she concedes the importance of social class in shaping the potential of individuals to capitalize on these changes.

Jamieson's analysis of relevant empirical studies has led her to suggest that within heterosexual relationships, 'creative energy is deployed in disguising inequality, not in undermining it' (Jamieson, 1999: 485). In doing this, many couples admit that their domestic labour is organized along traditionally gendered lines, yet claim that this is only temporary and is based on practical reasons. To this end, couples deploy 'self-deceiving diversionary cover stories of gender-neutral accidents of fate: 'she happens to like cooking and I'm no good at it' (Jamieson, 1998: 145). A study by Brannen and Moss (1991), found that working wives condone or misreport their husband's inadequate sharing of household chores, and in doing so create a 'false consciousness'. VanEvery's (1996) study of self-defined anti-sexist living arrangements was inspired by an interest in the ways that heterosexual women attempt to arrange their domestic lives to incorporate feminist critiques of the family. In these case studies, the male partners undertook the majority of household chores; however, they retained control of the relationship, and could change their minds at any time, which made their participation optional, unlike the taken for granted quality of women's domestic labour.

Irwin (1999) argues that theories of domestic labour tend to treat the domains of the social (the family) and the economic (the labour market) as distinct but interacting spheres that are driven by different dynamics (1999: 32). Irwin believes that the two are much more closely related, as individual's social locations are embedded in a structure of access to and rewards from employment. It is suggested that we are in fact witnessing a change in the relations of men and women because of women's increasing participation in the labour force and the decline of male breadwinner earnings. Although Irwin is optimistic about this change, she does not believe it supports theories of the family that present developments as a consequence of increasing individualization and detraditionalization. Irwin argues that this view is contradicted by the continued importance of family obligations, as can be illustrated by the work of Finch and Mason (1993).

Evidence of the gendered division of household labour in late modern Britain is important in any discussion of equality between men and women, yet is of limited value in an analysis of the pure relationship which is also defined by mutual disclosure and emotional equality. Duncombe and Marsden (1993: 1) maintain that increasing expectations of couple relationships insist that intimacy involves emotional action and work. However, they note that this is incompatible with the existence of a gender difference in emotional behaviour in relation to love and intimacy. This is illustrated by studies such as that by Brannen and Collard (1982, cited in Duncombe and Marsden, 1993), which documented women's disappointment with their husband's inability to share their thoughts and feelings. Duncombe and Marsden's own research attempted to explain the inter-relationships between the emotional and economic lives of sixty cohabiting and married couples. The majority of their female respondents felt that their male partners lacked 'emotional participation' in their relationships, and many women built an emotional life apart from their partners, through their children, employment and friendships with other women. Duncombe and Marsden argue that gender differences lead to differences in the way men and women value intimate emotion, and differences in their ability to 'do' intimacy in personal relationships (Duncombe and Marsden, 1993: 8). The persistence of a gendered division of emotional labour has in this way led to the social reproduction of separate emotional cultures for men and women.

Evidence for the democratization of intimacy is ambiguous at best, as it is impossible to conclude whether increasing rates of cohabitation and divorce reflect a profound commitment to personal relationships, or are indicative of the 'end' of the family and meaningful relationships. Gillies (2003) highlights the ideological underpinnings of these narratives of social change. She argues that those who adopt a demoralization standpoint tend to endorse a conservative agenda promoting values of responsibility and duty at the expense of social and economic inequities. Non-conventional family forms are vilified as the embodiment of moral decline and depicted as threats to the very structure of society. Although I would argue that this does not motivate the analysis of authors such as Bauman, it is perhaps true for other proponents of this perspective. Those who welcome individualization as offering greater egalitarianism in intimate relations generate a view of equality and justice that operates independently from wider structural constraints (Gillies, 2003: 16). The democratization of the family is hailed as a private, personal transformation, occurring in spite of the inequity and discrimination which characterizes the public sphere. For those who emphasize continuity, the lived reality of heterosexual relationships remains largely unchanged.

Existing empirical evidence suggests that lived heterosexual relationships reflect late modern ideals in limited ways. The proponents of detraditionalization often lack a grounding in empirical research that would provide a more accurate representation of social reality. Yet the various critiques of this approach should not detract from the invaluable contribution made by these theorists, who have 'injected debate and excitement into the field of families, intimacy and relationships in a way achieved by feminist theorists some twenty or thirty years previously' (Smart, 2007: 24).

Problematizing Heterosexuality

The research presented here focuses on couples living within heterosexual relationships, a characteristic that I wish to make explicit as heterosexuality as a category is rarely acknowledged or problematized. Diane Richardson (1996: 2) points out that heterosexuality is treated as an unquestioned paradigm, resulting in heteronormativity. Consequently, heterosexuality is accepted as the blueprint for all couple relations, including same sex relationships. For example, when talking of lesbian couples having children, it is assumed that one partner must be the mother, with the other taking the father's role, rather than seeing them as two mothers (Richardson, 1996: 4). Hawkes (1996) argues that sexual desire is largely regarded as a fundamental human characteristic which we fear could be problematic if not controlled. Heterosexuality therefore exists as the officially sanctioned 'normal' expression of sexual desire (1996: 6).

Carol Smart writes for the need to problematize heterosexuality. She argues that we now have 'a slow but growing recognition that white is an ethnic status – not a natural given – which is a norm against which the Other must be judged. We need a similar move in the field of heterosexuality/ies' (Smart, 1996: 171). Similarly, Stevi Jackson (1996b: 175) maintains that heterosexuality can be 'problematized by making it visible, challenging its privileged status and struggling to change it in practice'. Heterosexuality has remained largely invisible in theories of households and families because it is assumed to be the natural precondition to childbearing (VanEvery, 1996: 44). Although allusions to sex are ubiquitous within late modern society, it is also regarded as an act of individual intimacy driven by biology hence the reluctance of some researchers to focus on it within a sociological context. However, the changes within expressions of sexuality documented over the past few decades, and within a wider historical context, suggest that human sexualities are shaped by much more than nature and are a relevant and important area of sociological inquiry.

The definitions of 'sex' and 'sexuality' are also problematic. At the most basic biological level, sex refers to the physical act itself, or to the possession of the relevant genitalia or chromosomes, which in turn are believed to shape male and female sexualities. However, Hawkes explains that these meanings have a social origin. Her understanding is that if sexuality exists simply as an expression of sexual desire, then the connection between sex and gender would be severed (1996: 8). Judith Butler (1990) has also illustrated the fragility of hegemonic heterosexuality which has to be continually acted out to maintain its existence. Interpretations of sexuality clearly have a socially constructed element which need to be explored and understood as well as acknowledged; 'sexuality is both a fiction and a reality, an artificial creation and a lived experience' (Hawkes, 1996: 8).

The emergence of heterosexuality as a concept is relatively recent, as sexuality is often regarded as a nineteenth century creation (Hawkes, 1996: 8). Evidence suggests that the taken for granted notion of the existence of two 'opposite' sexes is a modern phenomenon (Hawkes, 1996: 7). Sex and sexuality in the pre-modern European context, which spanned over 1400 years from the ancient Greeks until the dawn of Enlightenment thought in the seventeenth and eighteenth centuries, were conceptualized in a radically different manner to our understandings today (Lacquer, 1990). Within the context of late modernity, sexuality is regarded as a lifestyle choice, in which we engage through the reflexive project of the self (Giddens, 1991: 9). For Giddens, sexuality is now severed from reproduction and the 'rule of the phallus' (1992: 2), resulting in the emergence of 'plastic sexuality'. Giddens defines plastic sexuality as 'sex detached from its age old subservience to differential power' (1992: 147). From Giddens' analysis, one can ascertain that sexuality is no longer ruled by traditional constraints or biology, rather it is an aspect of the self that has to be explored and developed rather than assumed; indeed, 'in modern social life, self-identity, including sexual identity, is a reflexive achievement' (Giddens, 1992: 147).

The feminist debate has been particularly important in informing and challenging notions of sexuality and gender and influences the conceptualization of heterosexuality presented here. By taking an essentialist view of men as oppressors and women as victims, some radical feminists have moved towards the idea that women are naturally superior to men. A further problem with radical feminist theorizing of heterosexuality is that it tends to ignore the ways in which sexuality is constructed in our individual subjectivities (Jackson, 1996c: 24) and makes little allowance for agency. While gender differences are reproduced through heterosexual relationships, this is not always inevitable, as every relation is 'a site of potential change as much as it is a site of reproduction' (Hollway, 1996: 99). Smart (1996: 165) expresses concern with the ways in which some feminists view heterosex as the defining element of female oppression. She argues that by doing this, radical feminists unintentionally bolster male power and privilege. Smart offers a more contextualized reading, in which there are multiple meanings attached to different sexualities at the same time. Through her writing, Smart deconstructs the 'mythic status of unitary, transhistorical heterosexuality', and writes of 'heterosexualities and the diverse and competing meanings associated with and deriving from these heterosexualities' (1996: 166).

Many of the reactions to the radical feminist critique of women's heterosexual desire as for erotic domination by men have been defensive. Male writers have attempted to disown masculinity, or to argue that not all heterosex is based on domination and control (Robinson, 1996: 112). Similarly, heterosexual feminists, such as Hollway (1996), have argued that male and female partners can meet as equals. Hollway (1996: 105) maintains that 'mutual recognition' is possible within contemporary heterosexual relationships, and creates the condition for egalitarian love and heterosex. Although I feel that the interpretation of heterosexual desire as inevitably based on the eroticization of the power difference is oversimplified, while women continue to be discriminated against one could claim that it is doubtful that men and women can enjoy a truly equal sexual relationship. Ideals of egalitarian sexual practices are undoubtedly more problematic for heterosexual couples because of the intrusion of gender differences (Sinfield, 2004). Hollway's ideal of two partners meeting as equals is reminiscent of Giddens' 'pure relationship' (1991, 1992), for which there is limited evidence. As Sinfield (2004) argues, we cannot simply sidestep hierarchies of male dominance. Sociological research suggests that power imbalances remain in heterosexual relationships, for example and 'institutionalised heterosexuality' is not limited to the physical act of sex. Jackson (1996c: 35) notes that heterosexuality is founded as much on men's access to women's unpaid labour as it is on access to women's bodies. These points encourage a broader view of heterosexuality and a need to analyse all of the practices that it encompasses, for example the naturalization of heterosexuality within government policy. Carabine (1996: 72) demonstrates the role of social policy as an instrument of disciplinary power, which continues to encourage female dependency on men.

Although the radical feminist argument has served to problematize heterosexuality, it has failed to engage in the positive aspects of pleasure (ibid). It could also be argued that the 'all or nothing' approach has alienated many young women from feminism, as Naomi Wolf's (1990) popularity indicates that it is unrealistic to expect them to choose academic theories over intimate relationships, and that many women within heterosexual relationships are 'far from being the dupes of patriarchy' (Smart, 1996: 177). As it is, the feminist debate has reached an impasse, which it needs to move beyond, through a new language that avoids the terms 'collusion' and 'collaboration' (Smart, 1996: 177). I would support Smart in her efforts to move the debate forward without falling back into the 'familiar retrenched positions' (Smart, 1996: 170). As she maintains, the challenge is to fragment the hegemonic heterosexual identity, 'and yet retain a politics and pleasure in more fragmented heterosexualities' (Smart, 1996: 174).

From a historical perspective, the emergence of Giddens' 'plastic sexuality' reflects the popular view that sex and sexuality have become increasingly liberated over the last century. Foucault recognized a more complicated process of continuity, rather than change. Hawkes argues that approaches that stress this, rather than relying on contrasts, can better illustrate existing sexual ideologies and the ways in which they are connected to past ideals (Hawkes, 1996: 32).

Through the appreciation of different experiences and the recognition that there are a number of heterosexualities, we can allow for 'the element of pleasure in heterosexual practices' (Segal, cited in Smart, 1996: 175) and at the same time problematize the idea of hegemonic heterosexuality. To quote Smart (1996: 177), 'we still know virtually nothing about how women in non-abusive relationships are negotiating their sexuality'; one of the aims of this research is to contribute to this endeavour.

Masculinity

The previous section's discussion focused almost exclusively on female heterosexuality, as sociology has only recently begun to unpack and problematize masculinity as a concept. As this study interrogates the experiences of both male and female partners, the ways in which heterosexual masculinities are constructed and regulated also have to be explored. To do this, one must first have a clear understanding of what 'masculinity' actually is. Masculinity tends to be something that is taken for granted and therefore is not easy to articulate, as until recently, women have been perceived as mysterious and in need of explanation, while masculinity has been represented as natural and normal; 'Not long ago woman was still the dark continent of humanity, whereas no one dreamed of questioning man' (Badinter, 1995: xll).

The idea of masculinity as a purely biological phenomenon has been dismissed within sociology, with the growing recognition that if femininity is a social construct then men are also located in specific cultural forms (Mac an Ghaill and Haywood, 2007: 29). In this way, masculinity is historically and culturally located and the search for a transcendent, timeless phenomenon is fruitless (Kimmel, 2001: 277). Masculinity is also not to be understood as a single, unified object of study, but as a plurality (Morgan, 2001: 224). On an individual as well as social level, masculinity is a constantly changing collection of meanings, constructed through relationships with the self, others and the world (Kimmel, 2001: 266). While we wish to believe in a universal and permanent principle of masculinity which defies time, space and the life course (Badinter, 1995: 1) masculinities exist in the plural and interact with race, social class, location, age and sexuality.

Connell notes that masculinity is concerned with public conventions, but that these conventions are not passively internalized and enacted, but are made and remade within social practice itself (Connell, 1995: 68). From this perspective masculinity is not understood as a coherent object, as it only exists in contrast to femininity (ibid). Factors such as race, social class and sexuality highlight the need to recognize multiple masculinities, however, Connell identifies what he terms 'hegemonic masculinity' as the dominant form of masculinity, which is defined as 'the configuration of practice which embodies the currently accepted answer to the problem of the legitimacy of patriarchy, which guarantees (or is taken to guarantee) the dominant position of men and the subordination of women' (Connell, 1995: 77). Hegemonic masculinity has cultural and institutional dominance, as it is exalted above all others at a particular point in time, and is sustained by the most powerful groups in society. Rather than constituting a fixed character type, hegemonic masculinity is fluid, and may differ through time and place. Although the majority of men do not embody hegemonic masculinity, they do benefit from its dominance in terms of prestige and power. The identification of a hegemonic masculinity is particularly important within this research, as the male participants are white and middle-class and therefore have a 'relationship of complicity with the hegemonic project' (Connell, 1995: 79).

While Connell maintains that no form of femininity achieves hegemonic status, he describes an 'emphasised femininity' (Connell, 1987: 187), which is fundamentally compliant with the dominance of men, through displays of sociability rather than competence, and the acceptance of marriage and childcare as a response to gender inequality within the workplace. The relationship between masculinities and femininities and how this manifests within heterosexual relationships is a key theme of this research, as Connell notes the importance of understanding the 'state of play' (Connell, 1987: 120) between the two.

I would argue that it is not possible to define masculinity as something that belongs to men, or is an inherent part of them, as I understand masculinity as a social construction that varies over time and place. Rather than a simple shift from traditional to modern forms of masculinity, complex structures of gender relations are apparent, in which 'dominant, subordinated and marginalized masculinities are in constant interaction, changing the conditions for each other's existence and transforming themselves as they do' (Connell, 1995: 198). It is interesting to note that accounts of masculinity are located firmly within the public sphere. The emergence of dominant ideals of masculinity appears to have accompanied the growth of capitalism, which perhaps accounts for this. The concern here is with the intimate relationships in which men find themselves, something that has come under public scrutiny over the past few decades.

The development of a woman-centred perspective has shed light on masculinity and men, as for the first time in history, men cease to represent the norm and become objects of study (Mac an Ghaill and Haywood, 2007). Radical and socialist feminists have pointed out that equal rights legislation is not sufficient to give women an equal starting point in society, as underlying structures are organized around men's interests (Edley and Wetherall, 1995: 175). Feminist identification of the personal as the political has also drawn attention to power imbalances within intimate relationships. Research conducted by Pamela Ashman in 1978 revealed that within heterosexual relationships, men monopolize conversational space by interrupting women and talking for longer periods, leaving women with 'the shit work of conversation' (cited in Edley and Wetherall, 1995: 183). Patriarchy, therefore, not only structures the public sphere, but also structures peoples' consciousness and interaction.

This early feminist argument has since come under attack from several angles. Segal (2001) writes that such arguments actually bolster male power, by 'endorsing myths of the inevitable link between sexuality and male dominance' (Segal, 2001: 108). Segal argues that most men experience their greatest uncertainties and anxieties through heterosexual sex and that it is deterministic and monolithic to suggest that male sexuality is a single shared experience. Connell (1995) maintains that neither men nor women are homogenous groups, although certain groups do manage to control dominant forms of masculinity. It has also been suggested that although the term 'patriarchy' has a political sharpness, 'gender' is a better tool for analysis as it is less deterministic (Arber, 1989).

The response of men to feminist critiques has been varied. Many men have rejected feminist theories, which can be illustrated by the 'men's rights' movements. The Mythopoetic men's movement, characterized by Robert Bly's *Iron John* (1990) bewails the powerlessness of modern men and tries to help men discover the warrior within (Kimmel, 2001: 283). This has proved especially appealing to privileged, white, heterosexual men (Edley and Wetherall, 1995: 199), and goes some way towards explaining the popularity of films such as Ridley Scott's *Gladiator* (2000). What the proponents of men's rights neglect to acknowledge is the fact that men remain in power, collectively if not individually (Kimmel, 2001: 283).

A second response by men to feminism is the anti-sexist movement, of which the journal 'Achilles Heel' is an example. However, as Segal points out, men do not have enough reason to change. A study of power imbalances within heterosexual relationships (Dallos and Dallos, 1997: 124) revealed that many of the women interviewed did not want to be seen as feminists, as if by becoming a feminist, a woman is seen as losing her feminine qualities. Dallos and Dallos argue that women as a group have been divided into 'feminist' or 'normal' women, which may be part of a reaction of male resistance to the threat feminism poses to their dominance. This response to feminism appears to be more sinister than reactionary men's rights movements, as it is less obvious, yet it has appeared to diffuse the influence of feminist arguments.

Psychoanalytic interpretations of masculinity have proved influential, as childhood is identified as the time when gender patterns are laid down. Freud believed that becoming human involved a conflict between a child's drives and the inhibitors that arise from interaction with parents and others (Edley and Wetherall, 1995: 41). During a boy's Oedipal stage, between the ages of three and five, he becomes aware of his penis and moves from his mother to the world of his father. Freud saw men as the superior sex as he interprets masculinity as the more secure gender identity. More recently, however, Freud's arguments have been reinterpreted. Nancy Chodorow (cited in Eisenstein, 1984) argues that girls grow up better adjusted than boys, who are constantly struggling against the feminine because of their initial identification with the mother. Men therefore grow up with a particularly fragile sense of gender identity, and masculinity forms as a defence. Kimmel (2001: 274) argues that the flight from femininity has three consequences; firstly a man pushes away his mother and the nurturing traits that she embodies. He goes on to suppress these traits within himself through fear that they will reveal his incomplete separation with his mother. Finally, he learns to devalue all women in society, as they embody the traits he has learned to despise. Masculinity is therefore founded on fear. Because the preoedipal boy sees the world through the eyes of his mother, he sees his father with a mixture of fear, awe and desire. Later on, men suppress this homoerotic desire, an act that results in homophobia (Kimmel, 2001: 276). Kimmel argues that peace of mind will only accompany a politics of inclusion, equality and justice.

Hollway (1996) argues that relationship patterns are social in origin, but also indicate the operation of the unconscious and the irrational. Although men are unlikely to voice their needs, they desire intimacy as much as women do (Hollway, 1996: 93). Drawing on the work of Foucault, Hollway suggests that there are three main discourses that construct both male and female identities. The 'male sexual drive' discourse (1996: 86) is particularly influential in the production of meanings concerning sexuality. Within this discourse, men present themselves as driven by biology; consequently male sexuality is presented as an impersonal need. The 'have/hold' discourse (Hollway, 1996: 86) emphasizes commitment and monogamy. Women are seen as the subject of the discourse, and men as the object; in other words, men position themselves outside of the discourse, as women strive to obtain commitment. Finally, the 'permissive' discourse (Hollway, 1996: 87) portrays sex as a matter of pleasure, as both men and women are entitled to free sexual expression. This discourse is perhaps more beneficial to men as it enhances their 'rights' to sex without having to make an emotional commitment. Hollway argues that these discourses socialize men and women into very different roles, which protect male power and repress the needs that men share in common with women. As a consequence, men project their weakness and dependency onto their female partner, as although the emotions belong to them, they are unacceptable. Within heterosexual relationships, emotions and roles become specialized, as the male partner may take the role of being independent and strong, while the female partner's role involves her being weak and emotional. The psychoanalytical approach retains its influence, however it has a tendency to assume that the nuclear family is a universal experience, and fails to account for individual differences and structural factors such as social class and ethnicity (Edley and Wetherall, 1995: 67). Psychoanalysis also reduces the economic, political and social structures that underlie the subordination of women to the private struggles of individual men and fails to identify the origin of women's devalued status (Eisenstein, 1984: 98).

Sex role theory explains social behaviour as a performance. From this perspective, masculinity is seen as an act, rather than an essence, which all men have to learn in order to perform (Edley and Wetherall, 1995: 71). In the 1970s, writers such as David and Brannon and Farrell (cited in Edley and Wetherall, 1995: 81) interpreted the male role as limited and constricting and potentially dangerous for men themselves and others, for example, women and the environment. The role theory is appealing as it appears to tap into common sense and it accounts for historical and cultural change. However, it is deterministic and oversimplifies the problem of masculinity, by assuming that men neatly slot in to the roles on offer. Connell (1995: 26–27) argues that sex role theory focuses exclusively on middle class, white masculinity, and that the structure behind it is biologically based, on male or female, rather than defined by social relations. The sex role theory has failed to generate a strategic and comprehensive politics of masculinity (Connell, 1995: 27).

The social constructionist perspective is the approach favoured here as it recognizes that gender is not fixed in advance of social interaction, but is constructed in interaction (Connell, 1995), thus recognizing the contradictory and dynamic character of gender. As Connell (1995: 39) argues, other approaches have failed to construct a coherent science of masculinity because masculinity is not a coherent object, which is recognized by this perspective. If masculinity is socially constructed, we have to identify where it is located (Edley and Wetherall, 1995: 210), from this approach masculinity is located in history, as it is not something someone is, but something that someone does. Therefore if we are doing gender, rather than attempting to define masculinity as an object, we need to focus on the social processes and relationships through which individuals conduct gendered lives (Connell, 1995: 71). Morgan (2001: 230) suggests that intimate relationships are an important site where we 'do' gender, as masculinities are not passively available, but are open for further elaboration and creation.

Badinter (1995) describes the insecurity felt by many men, who have to acquire their masculinity, unlike women who have physical proof of their femininity with menstruation, men have to work at 'being a man' (Badinter, 1995: 2). In this way, manhood is not bestowed at the outset, rather it is constructed or manufactured, and is therefore fallible. Badinter quotes Bourdieu, who stated 'to praise a man, one has only to say "he's a man"' (Badinter, 1995: 2). As masculinity is a relational concept, the changes in femininity have destabilized traditional notions of masculinity, and Badinter notes that it is not clear yet which types of masculinity that will emerge.

Recognizing masculinity as a social construct does not mean that it can be straightforwardly changed, as the material structures supporting patriarchy remain firmly in place. Ideologies and discourses are influential in shaping male behaviour, as men have traditionally grow up learning that they should be independent and unemotional (Mac an Ghaill and Heywood, 2007). Harris (1995) identifies several messages that influence the way men construct their own identities. Within intimate relationships, these dominant messages are the breadwinner, the nurturer, the faithful husband, and the playboy (Harris, 1995: 90–106). Although these are the dominant messages, Harris notes that specific cultural groups provide different lenses and different understandings of masculinity. Particularly relevant for this study is the generational lens (Harris, 1995: 164), as men raised in different time periods may have different values. Yet the changing nature of gender relations suggests a fundamental shift in social roles and the destabilization of traditional constructions of masculinity which should be apparent in the ways that the younger male participants discuss their relationships.

Generation as a Social Category

As the focus of this book is a study of the experiences of and attitudes towards pair relationships of two generations of heterosexual couples, it is necessary to clarify what is meant by 'generation' and the ways in which it has been sociologically conceptualized and theorized. The advantages of cross-generational sampling are evident in other research on couple relationships, most notably Lewis (2001) and Hockey, Robinson and Meah (2002). In her study of marriage and cohabitation, Jane Lewis interviews a younger sample of twenty-nine couples with dependent children, and compares their findings to those of their parents. Hockey, Robinson and Meah (2002) conducted a major study of heterosexuality and ageing, sampling three generations of respondents from twenty families from a range of backgrounds.

Age and generation have been largely neglected within British sociology, both theoretically and empirically (Pilcher, 1994: 482). Beh (1996) points out that generation remains the 'ugly sister' of more accepted social aggregates, such as social class. This may be because the ways in which age and generation are socially constructed has only recently been acknowledged. In the west, age is conceptualized numerically, reflecting the chronological measurement of calendar time. However, Pilcher (1995: 1) describes age as a social category, through which individuals are defined and identified, as although age has an obvious biological basis, its significance is socially constructed. Age is also located in historical time, as the period of history through which an individual lives shapes their experiences and defines the generation that they belong to. Age and time are structured differently according to gender, as women's time is used and conceptualized in a different way to men's time (Nowotny, 1994). Pilcher goes on to define the term 'generation'. The popular conceptualization of 'generation', meaning a group of people who experienced or took part in the same historical event, for example the 'War generation', is erroneous, as generation refers to kinship relations, or more specifically, the parent-child relationship (Pilcher, 1995: 6). 'Cohort' is the demographic term that refers to 'a defined population who experience the same significant event in a given period of calendar time' (Pilcher, 1995: 6), and is used most frequently to describe people born in the same year or decade.

Social theorists have attempted to explain age and generation from a number of perspectives, however, Mannheim's essay, written and originally published in 1923, remains 'the seminal theoretical treatment of generations as a sociological phenomenon' (Pilcher, 1994: 481). Mannheim uses the term 'generation' in the sense of cohort, and in sensitivity to this, Pilcher places the word 'social' before generation when discussing his work (Pilcher, 1995: 23). Mannheim's theory is based on the premise that youth is a key period of exposure, which has lasting effects, and as a consequence, during youth each generation develops a distinctive historical consciousness. Although several generations may be contemporaneous, they experience and interpret events differently, according to their unique historical location. Mannheim is more concerned with social processes than with biological considerations, and he explains that sharing a date of birth does not in itself involve similarity of location, as 'mere contemporaneity becomes sociologically significant only when it involves participation in the same historical and social circumstance' (Mannheim, 1952: 289).

According to Mannheim's theory, the two generations of respondents to this study will have experienced many of the same events, but in different and irreconcilable ways as a result of their distinctive worldview, which is shared only by members of the same generation. Mannheim argued that one's location within a social generation is similar to location within the class structure, as it points to certain modes of behaviour (Pilcher, 1995: 138), although, unlike social class, generation is not something that is open to agency, as it remains fixed throughout an individual's life. Mannheim's theory of generations is essentially a theory of complex social change, as social generations are regarded as a key element of such change (Pilcher, 1995: 139). The progression of change is made smoother by the emergence of intermediary, 'buffer' generations. However, Mannheim maintained that such progress is not straightforward; 'not only does the teacher educate his pupil, but the pupil educates his teacher too. Generations are in a state of constant interaction' (Mannheim, 1952: 301).

The Study

The aim of the research presented here is to interrogate the experiences and expectations of individuals within dyadic heterosexual relationships and ascertain the extent to which they reflect the dominant sociological accounts, detailed earlier in this chapter. A major challenge of designing the study was choosing a methodology which would be flexible and sensitive enough to evaluate what it means to be part of a couple. A qualitative approach was selected as the most appropriate method of investigation, with the focus on a richness of data rather than statistical information. Plummer (1995) explains that researchers uncover 'stories' from their respondents, with story-telling understood as a key way in which people make sense of themselves and the wider social world. The stories that the participants constructed about their relationships were a key focus of this research and while not necessarily fictional, they are constructed and are not assumed to be accurate reflections of an objective reality. Stories are valuable, not as mere resources, but as topics of investigation in their own right (Plummer, 1995: 12) as subjectivity exists not only in the telling, but also in the reading as there may be multiple interpretations of a single story with no way with which to identify the 'correct' reading. For example, my own interpretations of my respondents' testimonies may differ from those of another researcher. As a result, qualitative researchers use interviews as an opportunity to explore the subjective meanings that positivists attempt to eliminate from their data (O'Connell Davidson and Layder, 1994: 121). While being cautious not to overstate the capacity of the findings, this study makes an important contribution to an under-researched area by illuminating the discourses and ideologies couples may draw on to make sense of their relationships, without making universal claims about the reality of the heterosexual pair relationship.

The research took the form of semi-structured interviews and focus groups conducted with two samples of heterosexual couples The larger sample, which forms the central focus of the research was made up of twelve dual-career cohabiting couples aged between twenty and thirty-five without dependent children, with an additional sample of five couples aged between fifty and sixty-five. Each partner was interviewed individually, face to face. The interviews were supplemented with three focus groups conducted with a number of the willing interviewees. Intimate relationships are regarded as intensely private (Gabb, 2010), which made recruiting respondents particularly difficult, although the research is rendered more valuable through its illumination of what may be seen as an area of life that is usually 'off-limits' to outsiders. The ethical issues associated with researching a sensitive topic are numerous, and may involve potential costs to the respondents (Lee and Renzetti, 1993). A major concern was that in the interviews the participants were forced to reflect upon their own relationships and the possibility that taking part in the research may have been a catalyst for the dissolution of two of these relationships shortly after the study ended.

Using a purposive sampling strategy, the younger cohort was selected as theoretically this is the section of the adult population in Britain that is most likely to have been influenced by the ideology of the pure relationship, with its emergence dated to the 1960s (Giddens, 1992). Although the desired cohort was aged between twenty and thirty-five, in practice the majority of participants were in their late twenties to early thirties when they took part in the research. The older generation under study will also have lived through the emergence of the various ideologies and discourses centred on the couple relationships, however, they will have reached maturity at a point in history in which more traditional stereotypes of heterosexual relationships predominated. In this case, I wish to explore how far the older respondents' conceptualizations of relationships conform either to traditional or late modern ideologies, and whether they feel that their relationships have changed over time, in conjunction with the emergence of the pure relationship. In generational terms, my older respondents have a unique position, as they form part of the 'Baby Boomer' generation, or large cohort born post World War II, which is characterized by the growth of the new middle classes and a new set of values (Featherstone, 1989).

In limiting my sample to middle-class, heterosexual couples within certain age groups I was attempting to study a small selection of people with specific characteristics. Ensuring that the couples interviewed were not overly diverse was a strategy also used by Lewis (2001: 127), which, she argued, helped to confirm or deny her research hypothesis. I also followed Lewis's example of interviewing couples in intact relationships, which builds in a conservative bias (Lewis, 2001: 150). Difficulties in recruiting older couples resulted in a smaller sample of this cohort, meaning that analysis focuses on the larger younger sample. While the specific findings of this study are applicable only to the actual respondents interviewed, the individuals interviewed are not detached from wider social forces (Layder, 1994), and their testimonies reveal information about these forces, which may also influence other couples in similar relationships. As the characteristics of the two samples studied are so specific, they form the basis of tentative theoretical, if not empirical, generalizations (Mason, 2002: 195). While cautious not to overstate the capacity of the findings, they will make a contribution to an under-researched area by illuminating the discourses and ideologies which influence the participants. The shortcomings of the chosen methodology have to be acknowledged; I am interested in people's experiences, but in interviews these can only be recounted. Frith and Kitzinger (1998: 299) argue that interview data is 'talk-in-interaction' which is constructed in the interview context, rather than a 'transparent window' (1998: 304) through which we are able to view participants' actual experiences.

In order to gain a greater understanding of the shared understandings and definitions employed in reference to intimate relationships, focus groups were conducted based on divisions of gender and age/generation. Using focus groups enabled my research to focus on the ways in which experiences and opinions are formed through interaction (Morgan, 1994, 1997; Krueger and Casey, 2000). There are a number of specific ethical issues associated with focus groups, most notably privacy (Morgan, 1997). As the focus group members had previously taken part in individual interviews, I refer to them by random initials in each transcript, as without this there would be a danger that other members of the group could identify extracts from the interviews.

The Couples

All participants have been given pseudonyms to ensure confidentiality as far as possible, although I have included their age at the time of interview and occupation (in general terms). The couples are also numbered to facilitate identification of partners in the text, with the female partners identified as 'a' and the men as 'b'. Quotations are used in the text to substantiate arguments, and are edited for brevity, with the interviewer's speech highlighted in italics.

Couple 1: Jane (26, chartered accountant) and Ian (26, hospital doctor) began their relationship while at university, and have been cohabiting for five years.

Couple 2: Kate (27, probation officer) and Sam (27, company director) began their relationship while at university, and have been cohabiting for six years. They separated shortly after taking part in the study.

Couple 3: Anna (28, hospital doctor) and Carl (29, hospital doctor) began their relationship six years ago while training at the same hospital. They have been cohabiting for four years.

Couple 4: Carrie (27, researcher) and John (27, programmer) began their relationship while at university, and have been cohabiting for six years.

Couple 5: Christie (29, general practitioner) and Niall (30, general practitioner) began their relationship while working together eight years ago, and have been cohabiting for six years. They are engaged to be married.

Couple 6: Ali (26, customer service manager) and Ben (26, IT consultant) began their relationship while at university, and have been cohabiting for five years. They separated shortly after taking part in the study.

Couple 7: Dawn (28, chartered accountant) and Jeff (29, chartered accountant) began their relationship nine months ago after meeting at work. They have been cohabiting for six months.

Couple 8: Michelle (25, public relations advisor) and Mark (29, company owner) began their relationship after meeting through friends five years ago. They have been cohabiting for three years and are engaged to be married.

Couple 9: Chloe (24, accounts manager) and Paul (27, manager) began their relationship after meeting at work three years ago. They have been cohabiting for two years.

Couple 10: Sara (29, recruitment consultant) and Stephen (31, journalist) began their relationship after meeting through friends four years ago. They have been cohabiting for three years.

Couple 11: Emma (31, lab technician) and Phil (34, executive) began their relationship seven years ago. They have been cohabiting for six years and are engaged to be married.

Couple 12: Teresa (28, classical musician) and Alex (29, programmer) began their relationship after meeting through friends three years ago. They have been cohabiting for two years.

Couple 21: Fiona (56, housewife) and Trevor (55, managing director) have been married for thirty years and have two adult sons.

Couple 22: Marie (55, housewife) and Anton (63, retired airline captain) have been married for thirty-one years and have two adult children.

Couple 23: Anne (50, works part-time in the public sector) and Patrick (52, retired company director) have been married for twenty-nine years and have four adult daughters.

Couple 24: Liz (53, housewife) has been married for twenty-eight years, after initially agreeing, her husband refused to take part in the study. They have two adult children.

Couple 25: Barbara (54, housewife) and Richard (59, managing director) have been married for twenty-eight years and have two adult sons.

Summary

This chapter has located the study within the theoretical context that it is informed by. While the research this book is based on is necessarily small scale, the themes it addresses are not and it is possible that various issues will not be given the space that they warrant. Nevertheless, this work is designed as an empirical contribution to sociological understandings of the ways in which dyadic heterosexual relationships are experienced and understood by their members. The conflicting interpretations of the contemporary state of intimate relationships highlight the methodological difficulties of researching this topic, as each approach views intimacy through a particular ideological lens which fixes the parameters for comprehension and explanation (Gillies, 2003). For Gillies, this complexity points to the importance of grounded, contextualized studies of personal relationships and it is within this endeavour that these findings will make their most valuable contribution. The following chapters address the major themes which emerged from the findings; commitment, work and finances, housework, sex, love and lifestyle.

Chapter 2
Being Committed:
Making the Decision to Embark
on a Long-term Relationship

The causes of relationship breakdown have become a major focus of academic and public policy research, however, less attention has been paid to the motivations of individuals to commit to a long-term partnership. In this first empirical chapter the process through which the participants embark on and commit to being in a dyadic heterosexual relationship is examined. The findings suggest that while respondents explicitly reject the idea of selecting a partner on the basis of traditional obligations such as social class and economic security, in practice financial benefit, practical convenience, timing and compatibility based on lifestyle choices were cited as the most common reasons for committing to a long-term relationship. For the younger couples commitment was generally defined as making the decision to cohabit, with buying a house seen as particularly significant. For the older couples deciding to marry was of more significance, as it preceded living together. The research produced little evidence of commitment being dependent on intense communication and mutual self-disclosure, as posited by Giddens (1992), with most of the couples interviewed conforming more to Evans' (2003) description of modern partnerships based on shared tastes and convenience.

Defining Commitment

Commitment is a nebulous term whose meaning differs according to context. As the focus here is on intimate couple relationships I attempt to define it accordingly. The decline in marriage and increasing rates of divorce and single parenting would suggest that commitment to couple relationships has been undermined. However, perhaps now more than ever before, the couple relationship is regarded as 'the most significant and central personal relationship in both public stories and everyday practices' (Jamieson, 1998: 136). With marriage rates at an all-time low (Office for National Statistics, 2011a) forms of commitment may have changed for couples; Barlow et al. (2005) note that cohabitation may be underpinned with increased levels of dedication because of the lack of formal and legal binds. While commitment has become an established public and political concern, Smart (2007) notes that it has also emerged as a key theme in the sociological debate over the impact of individualization on intimate relationships.

Within the context of Giddens' pure relationship commitment is negotiated and contingent and comes without the guarantees of traditional ties such as marriage. Instead, 'it is a feature of the pure relationship that it can be terminated, more or less at will, by either partner at any particular point' (Giddens, 1992: 137). Similarly, Beck and Beck-Gernsheim propose that young people seek 'emotional commitment' (1995: 16) while rejecting traditional notions of family and marriage, while Weeks (2007) maintains that commitments within contemporary relationships are now negotiated rather than obligatory. From a pessimistic perspective Bauman (2000) warns that the necessary compromise involved in true commitment is rendered impossible within late modern relationships which he characterizes as driven by personal satisfaction.

Jamison (1998) cautions against interpreting declining rates of marriage and the trend towards cohabitation as evidence that couples are less committed to their partnerships. While cohabiting relationships are more fragile than marriages, this is likely to be because they have fewer financial ties and less social support rather than because of a rejection of traditional forms of commitment (Jamieson, 1998: 156). Jamieson reminds us that cohabiting couples are not homogenous, a point which is explored in Smart and Stevens' (2000) research on the relationship break-down of cohabiting relationships. They argue that commitment should be understood as being on a continuum rather than as a fixed entity. This continuum has relationships based on a mutual bond at one end, with relationships based on contingent ties at the other extreme. A certain level of permanence is presumed within relationships toward the former end, with partners having discussed and agreed on the nature and meaning of their relationship, which is usually supported by financial arrangements. At the other end of the scale relationships based on contingent ties lack legal and financial anchors and are hoped rather than expected to be lasting in the manner of Giddens' pure relationship.

Jane Lewis (2001) also takes a nuanced view of commitment in her research on the relationships of cohabiting couples. She defines commitment as 'behaving in ways that support the maintenance and continuation of a relationship' (2001: 124), rejecting other definitions that focus exclusively on satisfaction or stability as too narrow. Lewis draws on Mansfield's idea that commitment has two components; commitment to the relationship which is personal and focused on the present and commitment to the partnership which is future-oriented and is crucial to long-term stability (1999, in Lewis, 2001: 125). Age and generation may influence what commitment means to couples. Sutton et al. (2003) found that commitment for older couples was based on traditionally gendered roles, involving elements of care and responsibility to one's spouse, while younger couples report commitment as a personal expression exempt from societal pressures.

Commitment is closely linked to power and control within relationships. If we are to understand commitment as a scale or continuum then we should also examine how couples progress along it. Much of the discussion on commitment presumes that couples are matched in their desire for commitment as relationships have come to be based on 'emotional give and take' (Giddens, 1991: 62) and an end to traditionally gendered roles which are renegotiated to give each partner an equal say. From the perspective that contemporary relationships are based on the principles of democracy and personal freedom commitment would be something that is mutually agreed upon, with both partners satisfied with the progression of their relationship. In an egalitarian relationship, both partners should be able to influence each other to the same extent, with neither partner having overall dominance (Dallos and Dallos, 1997: 13). However, research indicates that young women lack power in heterosexual dating relationships (Chung, 2005) which continue to be characterized by gender inequality.

Methodological Issues

The couples here were asked about how they viewed their relationships and why they decided to take steps to consolidate and continue their relationships. Commitment was happily discussed by all of the respondents and peppered the interview and focus group transcripts. With commitment linked to power and control, the research focussed on the balances of power displayed by my respondents within their relationships and their respective control over the forms that their relationships took. This was particularly difficult to evaluate as it is not easily quantifiable and depends heavily on the researcher's interpretation of what constitutes power. Craib (1994: 149) maintains that analysis of intimate relationships in terms of power is 'a great oversimplification of what goes on between people', however I would argue that power dynamics are key to understanding relationships as long as we take a nuanced view of what power actually is.

In an attempt to ascertain the balance of power within my respondents' relationships with regard to commitment I searched the interview transcripts for dialogue relating to these definitions of power. In an equal relationship, both partners should be able to influence each other to the same extent; if this is not the case then one partner holds more power than the other. Identifying what actually constitutes power is not the only methodological challenge I am faced with here; I also have to identify how the workings of power are revealed through what my respondents' say. Asking a straightforward question about who holds the most power in the relationship proved ineffective, for example, in the first interview I conducted, the female interviewee retorted:

> 'Oh, God, no, we're equal in terms of power. What kind of relationship would it be if one of you had more power than the other? We're not Victorians, you know.' (Jane, 1a)

The term 'power' appeared to hold negative connotations for Jane, perhaps as the idea that one partner explicitly holds more power than the other clashes with the late modern relationship ideal of equality; comparing herself to a Victorian reiterates her insistence that she is in a 'modern', equal relationship. However, in the course of the interview, Jane later explained that within her relationship with Ian;

> 'I think I'm like the secretary and he's like the managing director. I do all the practical stuff, but he always organises going out.'

Comparing the roles in the relationship to a gendered corporate hierarchy is a clear expression of the imbalance within the relationship, which has nothing to do with the partners' actual occupational status; while Ian is a doctor, Jane is an accountant at a major firm. The fact that professional status appears to have little relevance to the power resources within the relationship illustrates the latent power processes exercised by Ian and the discrepancy between the ideal of the pure relationship to which Jane aspires and the lived reality of their relationship as she describes it. The differences between 'dominant' and 'muted' discourses (Anderson and Jack, 1998) can be demonstrated here. Within the interviews, direct questioning about power and control resulted in defensiveness and denial, whereas general discussion of each partner's respective role in the relationship encouraged disclosure about power and control.

A basic definition of power is the ability to impose one's will on others, possibly in the face of resistance. Within my research I employed two approaches for the study of power in relationships, developed in previous sociological research on heterosexual relationships. The first is as defined by Dempsey (1998), who identifies two distinct, yet related types of power processes. 'Manifest' power processes are easily identifiable, as they are verbalized by the partners, and may be accompanied by overt negotiations or conflict, aimed at changing existing negotiations. 'Latent' processes are less obvious as they are unspoken and involve a partner anticipating what the other partner would like them to do, and then doing it.

Dallos and Dallos' (1997) descriptions of power within relationships provided a useful conceptual framework. They note the difference between 'structural' and 'ideological' power. Structural power refers to access to education, employment and physical strength, and has similarities with Dempsey's description of manifest power. Ideological power functions by shaping people's thinking about how relationships 'should be', in other words, discourse, and overlaps with Dempsey's latent power. While there are similarities between the two approaches to power, I feel that alone, neither Dallos and Dallos' nor Dempsey's definitions sufficiently encompass the multiple power processes at work within the relationships studied. Drawing from both approaches, I employ a definition of power that differentiates between power *resources* and power *processes*. Resources refer to the physical, structural and ideological power bases enjoyed by each partner, whereas power processes denote the less tangible workings of power. The ways in which power is discursively constructed is important here, as although each couple is unique, my research suggests that they rely on a limited number of discourses with which to construct their own personal narratives. As Foucault (1979) posited, societies construct a hierarchy of discourses, which shape our thoughts, experiences and interactions. While certain discourses are promoted and validated, others are undermined or sidelined. Power processes refer to the ways in which certain discourses may be used by my respondents to support their own or undermine their partner's authority.

Commitment and Control

Rather than impose an external definition of what commitment is on the participants, I sought to explore the ways in which they conceptualized it. In the focus groups held with younger male and female respondents I asked the participants to define commitment in a relationship:

So what does commitment actually mean in a relationship?
J – not seeing anyone else
M – yeah, but it's more than that, it means committing to a future together I would have said
Would the rest of you agree with that?
S – I think it's both really, it totally depends on what stage you're at in a relationship
J – totally, the kind of commitment you want when you've just started seeing each other isn't the same as what we've got now, with a house and mortgage
C – there are definitely stages in a relationship
What do you think the stages are?
J – well when you're just going out then it's like being exclusive
L – going on holiday was a big step early on

C – definitely that's make or break (group laughter)

M – then you've got like, meeting each other's parents, moving in, erm, then in your thirties marriage, children

C – I think buying a house is a much bigger commitment than marriage, for me anyway

J – definitely, that's a huge commitment

(Female focus group, 20–35)

The younger female focus group understood commitment as a series of stages, with each stage displaying an increasing investment in the relationship. While the early tentative steps may involve sexual fidelity and going on holiday together, commitment increases as the relationship progresses culminating in a shared mortgage to be potentially followed by marriage and children. The discussion suggests that commitment to a relationship is future-oriented, with participants describing stages they expect to reach as well as those they have arrived at. The male focus group came up with a similar definition of commitment as a series of stages or steps:

How would you define commitment in a relationship?

P – something women want (group laughter)

P – seriously, it totally depends on where you are in a relationship

C – definitely, commitment is like different steps

A – I would say it's like a sliding scale, you know you start with being faithful, then telling someone you love them, then maybe moving in

P – but it's always the man that has to take the next step, you always have to go first, even from the beginning of asking a girl out right up to proposing

S – I've definitely felt a lot of pressure to commit, like to buy a house together, – was really pushing for it.

P – Every relationship I've been in, the girl was always pushing for more, you know?

Why do you think that women are more keen?

P – Er, I think that's just a basic difference, they want security, you know?

S – true.

(Male focus group, 20–35)

While both focus groups displayed similar understandings of what constituted commitment, the discussions in the male focus group also indicated that the men felt that their relationships were more important to their partners. The concern with focus group data is that the presence of other participants as well as the researcher may prompt respondents to answer in a particular way. Suggesting a lack of concern about their relationships may have been for the benefit of the other men in the group, rather than an accurate portrayal of their true feelings. However, the idea that women desire commitment more than men was also evident in the interview data:

> 'I would have moved in sooner than that, but I think he was quite worried about living together.'
> *Why?*
> 'He's not keen on commitment. That's why we'll probably never get married (laughs).' (Jane, 1a)

> 'Women are the ones that want to get married and all that aren't they? You don't see gays in, er, monogamous relationships.' (Mark, 8b)

Mark uses the perceived promiscuity of gay men to support his own reluctance to commit to his partner, drawing on essentialist discourses about masculinity to argue that men have no desire to be in long term monogamous relationships. It appears to be largely up to the male partner to commit, as it is automatically assumed that women want a long term relationship thus placing them in a position of weakness. One female respondent describes her attempts to encourage her partner to propose to her:

> 'I don't want to put an ultimatum on it, you know, but we've been together since uni, and I'd like to get married at some point, so he knows I want him to propose.'
> *Couldn't you propose?*
> 'God, no, that is one of those things I think he should do. Besides he'd probably run a mile.' (Ali, 6a)

> 'She's been talking about getting married for years, but I don't know, I'm not ready really.' (Ben, 6b)

The differences in the power resources of Ben and Ali are evident through these excerpts. While Ali's desperation to marry is palpable, Ben is dismissive. The decision to marry appears to be his, particularly as she is waiting for him to propose rather than asking him to marry her, showing the influence that supposedly obsolete traditions retain over heterosexual relationships. Duncombe and Marsden (1993: 236) suggest that men's withholding of emotional validation may be a source of male power, and here I would argue that the younger male respondents' withholding of commitment may also be a source of power. The 'have/hold' discourse, as described by Hollway (1996: 86), which emphasizes commitment and monogamy is influential in my respondents' descriptions of their relationships. Women are seen as the subject of this discourse, as they strive to obtain commitment, with men as the object. While participants in the younger female focus groups acknowledged that they wanted commitment from their partners, they rejected these essentialist explanations:

Do you think women want commitment more than men?
J – well, usually, I would say
C – definitely I feel I'm the driving force
L – yeah, but I hate this, this kind of view that women are all out to trap men into relationships, it's just bullshit, men want commitment too they're just not allowed to talk about it in front of their mates
S – That's so true
J – I really hate it when they make jokes, like if you go to a wedding and everyone's like 'be careful, she's going to get ideas', I hate it
M – oh I know, it's so disrespectful, like you tricked him into moving in
J – exactly, I mean I want our relationship to go somewhere, but I'm not some psycho who's going to start poking holes in condoms, you know? (group laughter).
(Female focus group, 20–35)

The view that women are biologically primed to 'trap' men into relationships emerged as a dominant discourse shaping the participants' ideas about commitment. It functions to undermine women and bolsters male power. Yet the definition of commitment as a series of stages is strangely impersonal and refers more to the structural elements of a relationship (buying a house, getting married) than individual closeness; for example one of the focus group participants reports that 'telling someone you love them' is a marker of commitment, rather than actually being in love. Sociological analysis has moved away from viewing relationships as fixed entities in favour of 'doing' intimacy (Duncombe and Marsden, 1993) or 'intimate practices' (Jamieson, 2011). Intimate practices are defined as actions 'which enable, generate and sustain a subjective sense of closeness and being attuned and special to each other' (Jamieson, 2011: 1.2). While telling someone you love them or moving in with them may constitute intimate practices, there are multiple ways of doing intimacy that can strengthen commitment to a partnership. In chapter six notions of intimacy and love are explored, with all participants claiming to be in love with their partners regardless of gender which suggests that commitment is also emotional. In the interviews, respondents' descriptions of how their relationships progress are also more commonly characterized by a mutual sense of pragmatism rather than being driven by the female partner.

Stages of Commitment

If we continue with this conceptualization of commitment as a series of steps or stages then the younger couples were all roughly at the same stage in their relationships; they were all cohabiting, eight shared a mortgage and three of were engaged. In the course of the interviews I asked the respondents to describe how their relationship began:

> 'We were kind of, it's like, we were going out but it was like just casual kind of dating. We were having sex, we weren't like "let's have a relationship"' (Jane, 1a)

> *What made you decide to start a relationship with Kate?*
> 'Err, I don't know really, it just happened. My best friend at halls started seeing Kate's best friend so we just ended up together.' (Sam, 2b)

> 'We didn't really decide to start a relationship, it just kind of happened, you know it was casual at first and then here we are five years later.' (Ali, 6a)

> *What made you decide to commit to each other in a long term relationship?*
> 'Oh I don't think anyone sits down and has that discussion, like 'we're now committed to each other', it just happens gradually, you know you love each other but also you like each other and have stuff in common'. (Anna, 3a)

> 'I didn't set out to get a relationship. It started off as a one night stand and just carried on from there (laughs). Romantic, eh?' (Carrie, 4a)

> 'It wasn't planned, we hooked up in a club and it just went from there really.' (Alex, 12b)

The notions that their relationships 'just happened' recurs in participants' accounts. Rather than trying to trap their partners into a committed relationship, the female respondents are particularly nonchalant about the drift from a casual relationship, usually based on sexual compatibility, to a more lasting partnership. While this could be interpreted as evidence of a shift to the pure relationship which is free of expectations and external ties, further exploration suggests that the intense discussion and reflection necessary for this type of intimacy is also missing. The respondents' relationships are instead characterized by drift and progress along the commitment scale without a great deal of discussion or reflection:

'Oh I don't think anyone sits down and has that discussion, like "we're now committed to each other", it just happens gradually, you know you love each other but also you like each other and have stuff in common.' (Anna, 3a)

Why did you decide to stay together?
'I guess because we were friends first, but it's stood us in good stead, because after the first year the rush goes, and you actually have to like each other and have things to talk about. We have the same group of friends, and do the same things, so it's cool.' (Carrie, 4a)

'We got on well with each other, so it was more like a case of "why not?" than "why" we've stayed together.' (Niall, 5b)

The motivation to commit to a particular partner is usually described as based on compatibility, having a shared friendship group or things in common. None of the participants referred to passion or desire as driving their actions. The decision to cohabit, regarded as a key stage in the progression of a relationship, was also characterized by practicality:

Why did you decide to move in together?
'Well it wasn't like some massive decision, it just seemed to make sense after uni since we were practically living together anyway, you know we could share rent rather than paying for two places.' (Kate, 2a)

'It was definitely an active decision, it's not like we were sharing a house and everyone moved out, but it wasn't really a big deal.' (John, 4b)

What prompted you to buy a house together?
'God, with prices here it made sense to buy together I don't know how people even buy . . . '
So it was a financial decision?
'Obviously I wouldn't have done it if I wasn't committed, but , erm, yeah, that was definitely a big part.' (Carl, 3b)
Why did you and Stephen move in together?
'To be honest it wasn't a huge deal, I don't think we even talked about it, at the time I wasn't getting on with my housemates and, I kind of just ended up moving in to his flat really.'
So it didn't seem like a big deal?
'Nah, just made sense really, it's not like we were buying the place.' (Sara, 10a)

'Why did you decide to buy a flat together?'
'Er, we really wanted to get on the property ladder, we'd been renting together for a year and it's so much easier to get a mortgage together, it's one of the main benefits of being with someone (laughs).' (Emma, 11a)

While cohabitation was a viewed as a major step for the couples, in the most of the accounts it was entered into without a great deal of reflection or discussion. The practical nature of moving in together may mean that the reasons cited for this step are more pragmatic, as the excerpts from the interviews show cohabitation is often prompted by decisions external to relationship, for example wanting to move out of a shared house or a lease being up, rather than as a major emotional commitment to the relationship. Where John describes moving in with his partner as an 'active decision' he concedes that it was 'not a big deal'. Within the accounts there is a clear distinction between moving into rented accommodation together and buying a property, which is regarded as a greater commitment because of the financial implications. For most of the couples there are two levels of cohabitation as they try out living together in a rented property before committing to a joint mortgage. The joint salaries of dual earner couples are often necessary to enable them to buy a property, with Emma joking that qualifying for a mortgage is one of the main benefits to being part of a couple. The other major reason for moving in together, and progressing down the commitment continuum was timing, which featured heavily in respondents discussions. Three of the couples interviewed were engaged to be married, and timing also appeared to be a major factor in this decision:

Why did you ask Michelle to marry you?
'Obviously I love her to pieces, you know and it was about time really, we've been together for five years.' (Mark, 8b)
Why did you decide to propose to Emma?
'I kind of wanted to anyway, the timing seemed right, she was definitely ready because her sister and some friends had just got married, and you know we'd been together for ages.' (Phil, 11b)
So why are you and Niall getting married?
'We've been together since third year, and I'm thirty next month so its not like we've rushed into it.'
Was the timing important?
'Well, yeah, I mean we've been living together for so long, but now our friends are starting to get married, so it feels right. I always said I wanted to be married when I was thirty so it's worked out well (laughs).' (Christie, 5a)

In contrast to cohabitation marriage is regarded as a symbolic gesture and remains heavily loaded with gendered traditions. While the notion of a marriage proposal seems outdated in the context of cohabiting relationships, they remain important to the participants. The younger female focus groups discussed getting engaged:

> *'Would you consider proposing?*
> C – I might have to at this rate (group laughter). Seriously I've told him he has to propose by the time I'm thirty.
> *Isn't telling someone they have to propose the same thing?*
> C – Not at all, it's the man's job he just needs a shove.
> J – I would never propose, you need it to be their decision or you'd always be wondering.
> M – I think with all the work we put in then all they have to do is get down on one knee, it's not a lot to ask is it really?
> L – I'm not too bothered about getting married but you're right I'd definitely want that he, for him to go to the effort.'
> *(Female focus group, 20–35)*

While it remains up to the male partner to propose marriage (notwithstanding the pressure that may be applied by his partner) the decision to marry is within their control. The act of proposing is framed as an act of one partner relinquishing power to the other, which may explain male reluctance to pop the question. For the female focus group proposing represents a rare gesture of commitment to the relationship on the part of their partners; as one participant explains 'I think with all the work we put in then all they have to do is get down on one knee'.

For the respondents who were planning to marry, timing is cited as a key factor. In particular turning thirty seems to be a significant milestone in their expectations of their relationships. Thirty seems to be the age at which it is now appropriate to get married or 'settle down' and is statistically the average age that British women enter their first marriage (Office for National Statistics, 2011a). That thirty is the age at which a relationship 'ought' to progress is a view that was expressed by the women interviewed in particular and almost seemed like a deadline at which point relationships should become more serious and they should have something to show for years of dating. One participant described feeling that she should marry in order to keep up with her peers:

> 'I've never been a girly girl, into the white dress, never dreamt about my wedding or whatever, but sometimes I feel (pause) I feel like there's something wrong with me, like I can totally see us getting married in a few years just because all our friends are, even though we're not really that bothered.' (Carrie, 4a)

Weeks (2007) and Smart and Stevens (2000) have both highlighted the importance of life course in commitment, although for the participants interviewed here this was more rigidly attached to age and their expectations of what their romantic achievements should be at a particular point in their lives. This may explain the more relaxed descriptions of moving in together, as participants may have felt less pressure to commit in their twenties and were more content to let their relationships drift. At the end of each interview, I asked each of the younger respondents what they saw as the future of their relationships. While the respondents from the two couples who later ended their relationships (Kate and Sam, and Ben and Ali) expressed uncertainty, every other respondent referred to marriage and most mentioned the possibility of children:

> 'I think we'll get married, then hopefully children at some point.' (Dawn, 7a)

> 'I guess marriage and kids, but not for a while yet.' (John, 4b)

> 'Eventually, I suppose we'll get married.' (Alex, 12b)

> 'I would hope we'd get married and have kids, or what's the point?' (Anna, 3a)

These responses illustrate the narratives the interviewees use to construct their relationships, which are expected to culminate in marriage and potentially children. For my respondents, heterosexual relationships appear to have retained their links with traditional family forms. The ideal of romantic love appears to have a strong influence on their expectations, as the couples see their relationships as long term; the 'until further notice' (Giddens, 1992) ethos of the pure relationship appears to have little sway here. While statistics suggest that many of these couples may eventually end their relationships, their projections for the futures of their relationships illustrate the limits of reflexivity. Beck and Beck-Gernsheim (2002: 6) insist that 'certainties have fragmented into questions' as traditional guidelines have become obsolete, however these guidelines have retained their relevance for the couples interviewed here. Duncan (2011) suggests that social institutions constrain us, as although we may actively choose our partner, we are limited by the norms of our culture which means that we act through ideas of what relationships should entail. While roles may have altered slightly, with female partners working and the timing of events such as marriage and children may have shifted, the traditional heterosexual career remains an atavistic ambition for my younger respondents.

The Older Couples Discuss Commitment

The older couples interviewed had all been married for at least twenty-five years, and at most felt that at the time that they met cohabitation wasn't an option:

> 'We knew each other for about a year before he proposed, I was living with my parents and it was natural that if you loved each other you would get married, there was no question of it.' (Barbara, 25a)

> 'There were girls, you know who lived with their boyfriends before they got married, but I would never have done it, my mother would have killed me.' (Marie, 22a)

> 'There's no way you'd live together or have children without being married.' (Trevor, 21b)

For the older respondents marriage was the only acceptable context in which they could enjoy an openly sexual relationship and cohabit with their partner. It was generally viewed as a natural next step in a relationship and was generally entered into without a great deal of reflection or discussion:

> 'I decided that's who I wanted to spend the rest of my life with, that's someone I get on with and that was it.' (Trevor, 21b)

> 'It wasn't a big surprise, if you liked someone had been together for a while then it was expected you'd get engaged really.' (Barbara, 25a)

One of the older female respondents, Liz, expressed some regret over how lightly she had entered into marriage with her husband (who refused to take part in the research):

> 'Well he proposed, we'd only been going out a few months and I just thought "we get on, why not?". But being married is so different I wasn't ready at that age, I think it's much better now that you can see if you can live with someone first. I always tell my kids they should do that before they even think about marriage because you just don't know, everything changes.' (Liz, 24a)

As cohabitation did not represent a viable option for the older couples at the beginning of their relationships, marriage is seen as the next step and one that is taken readily. Lewis notes that 'once marriage became a choice and not a necessity, a much more conscious decision had to be made to enter into it' (2001: 144), an observation supported by this research.

Fear of Being Single

For a number of the women interviewed a certain social status was attached to being in a relationship and many displayed an aversion to being single. With the demographic shift towards single person households cultural representations of single women have changed to reflect their experiences (Macvarish, 2006: 1.1). However, the stigma associated with being a single woman (Sandfield and Percy, 2003) is evident in the interviews conducted with the female respondents:

> 'It sounds really crap, but just being able to show I'm able to get a boyfriend, I have someone who loves me, makes me feel better.' (Jane, 1a)

For Jane part of the appeal of being in a relationship is the public display of competence and desirability. Although she later draws on positive depictions of singleness from the HBO series *Sex and the City*, she was generally disparaging about other single women. Similarly, Christie draws on negative stereotypes of single women:

> 'I do feel more secure being in a relationship, living with someone, rather than being on my own with cats, you know, Bridget Jones style.' (Christie, 5a)

Being single here is linked to unflattering yet pervasive portrayals of single women living with pet cats as anti-social and misanthropic (Tipper, 2011: 88) or as the hapless Bridget Jones of Helen Fielding's (1996) novel. Single women were also referred to with condescension and pity by female respondents:

> 'I feel sorry for anyone who can't get a boyfriend, I mean, who is single, you know, because it's so much nicer to be in a relationship, with someone to share things with.' (Kate, 2a)

> 'I look at my single friends, and I'm so glad I have Phil, because they seem so desperate, always out speed dating, or whatever, waiting for a bloke to call, and I don't think I could cope with it.' (Emma, 11a)

Whereas women may have a lower standing and fewer power resources within their relationships, their social standing may be improved by having a boyfriend. The compromises that these participants make for their partners may be traded off against the social power that they gain by being in a relationship. For the women interviewed here, being in a relationship forms an important part of their identity, perhaps in the same way that work supports the masculine identities of the men interviewed. Single women are described using pejorative terms, such as 'desperate', and are regarded with pity. There is no acknowledgement that remaining single may be a choice made by young women, it is assumed that the desire to be in a relationship is universal. According to Sandfield and Percy, stigmatization and marginalization are still the defining features of single womanhood; 'Traditional discourses of the female life plot cast heterosexual romance and marriage as the ultimate success' (Sandfield and Percy, 2003: 476). It is evident that fear of being single is a motivating factor in the respondents' desire for a committed relationship. This was particularly true for the older female participants who recalled a fear of being 'left on the shelf' in their youth:

'There was a lot of pressure to marry. I was in my mid-twenties when I married, and that was late for me, that was considered late.' (Marie, 22a)

'Well as soon as you left school the race was on, you know at 21 I was worried about being left on the shelf, because all my friends if they weren't already married they were dating. Any man you went out with was a potential husband.' (Barbara, 25a)

Here, Barbara describes finding a potential husband as a 'race', suggesting a certain amount of competition between her peers as to who could get married first. The older respondent's preoccupation with marriage seems anachronistic as the younger couples are cohabiting, however, the fear of being single is similar. While for the older women interviewed, the benefits of marriage are clear (financial security, a father for their children) for the younger women, all of whom have careers and could easily support themselves, the appeal of being in a heterosexual relationship is not as obvious. In the focus group of younger women, security was reiterated as an important reason for being in a relationship:

J – I think women are more insecure, you know about our bodies, or whatever.
S – Men are definitely more confident.
J – Yeah, well I think that's represented, reflected in your relationship, you know I'm always worried that he might get bored and leave, whereas men don't think like that.
M – That's part of living together, without being married, you know, you don't have that security, there's less commitment.
L – We're committed.
M – Yeah, but if you're not married, he can walk out tomorrow, that's why we bought a house, even though it's like a practical thing, it kind of ties you together.
(Female focus group, 20–35)

Needing external ties, for example marriage or a mortgage, suggests that the participants have not achieved Giddens' pure relationship, which is based on disclosing intimacy rather than legal or financial bonds. However the economic power resources brought to the relationships are considerably greater for the younger women than for their mothers' generation, particularly as mortgages are joint which means that couples share an equal stake in their homes. That this power resource does not translate into equality within the power processes at work in heterosexual relationships is one of the concerns of this research, as the fear that 'he might get bored and leave' undermines female respondents' status within their relationships.

Summary

What is particularly evident from the data presented here is the enduring appeal of the couple relationship for both generations of participants. Meeting and falling in love with a member of the opposite sex is a basic expectation that respondents have of their lives and once a bond is established relationships are expected to become more committed as couples take steps to increase the permanence of their relationships. Other research has found that couples may move between greater and lesser ties in their relationships (Smart and Stevens, 2000; Barlow et al., 2005), however the couples here usually had a linear vision of how their relationships would develop, with each 'step' seen as further progression to a more secure and committed relationship. The research produced little evidence of commitment being dependent on intense communication and mutual self-disclosure, with most of the relationships drifting from one step to another, usually on the basis of convenience. The only exception to this was marriage for the younger couples, which have moved from being a necessity to a lifestyle choice, albeit one that is taken because of timing and life stage.

Carter (2010: 175) distinguishes between 'pull factors' and 'push factors' in the process of developing ties. Pull factors draw a couple together and are characterized by love, fidelity and monogamy. These usually precede push factors, which include internal and external investments and expectations and are motivated by not wanting the relationship to end. Within this model certain stages of a relationship will be reached before it can progress, which can be usefully applied to my participants' relationships which are also conceptualized as having consecutive steps. The steps are different for the younger and older cohorts, with marriage regarded as a necessity for the latter before they could realistically live together. This pattern was reversed for the younger couples, with marriage representing a symbolic gesture which usually follows an extended period of cohabitation. Yet for both generations, relationships take similar forms and are characterized by a drift into commitment. Definitions of the landmarks relationships are expected to reach may have been modified, however monogamous couple relationships continue to be a key feature of the participants' life plots. This is particularly true for the female respondents, with fear of being single featuring as a significant push factor motivating them to stay with their partners. Women were seen as striving for commitment, particularly in regard to marriage, which is now regarded as optional yet has taken on a new significance and is regarded as the ultimate declaration of commitment. While the pull factors drawing the couples together don't appear to be heavily gendered, the push factors keeping them together and propelling the relationship towards further commitment seem to weigh more heavily on the female participants, which places them in a more precarious position and bolsters the power base of their partners.

Relationships usually began casually, with few expectations of the future attached, however once partners had been together for a certain length of time it was generally expected that they would take certain steps to consolidate their partnerships. While the younger participants have more choices with regard to the form that their relationships take than the older cohort, what is striking is how similar their relationships are, with marriage expected to follow a period of cohabitation. It may be that optimistic theorists have overstated the impact of individualization on social change and individuals' capacity for reflexivity. Vanessa May's (2011) discussion of the importance of belonging in the relationship between self and society offers a more nuanced explanation, with belonging conceptualized as something that we 'have to keep achieving through an active process' (May, 2011: 372). From this perspective it could be argued that the participants have to keep reaffirming their commitment in order not only to bolster their sense of belonging to their relationships but also to their peer group more generally.

Chapter 3
Money Matters:
Work and Finances

Over the past fifty years there has been a major transformation of men and women's participation in paid employment, with the erosion of the male-breadwinner model in favour of dual-earner families. As a consequence, the relationship between men, women and work has been fundamentally altered (Mac an Ghaill and Haywood, 2007). The ways in which the couples negotiate their financial arrangements, in terms of how money is managed and the impact of paid employment on relationships is explored here. For the younger couples finances are generally equally balanced, with most respondents stressing the importance of maintaining economic independence, whereas the older couples tend to conform to a male-breadwinner model even where both partners work. While the older couples interviewed constructed their relationships in terms of a clear separation of home, for which the woman was responsible and work, which was the man's responsibility, the younger couples displayed more nuanced power relations with both partners working. However, respondents tended to prioritize the man's career above that of his female partner, with both male and female participants describing the male partner's job as more important regardless of position or salary, suggesting that the massive changes in gendered patterns of employment have not always worked to undermine patriarchal social structures.

Managing Money

Attention was given to the role of work and money in the respondents' relationships because the shift from the male breadwinner model to the dual-earner partnerships is marked and has been interpreted as evidence of the democratization of intimate relationships (Giddens, 1992). The economic dependence of women on their husbands has been interpreted as a key factor in perpetuating inequality (Dryden, 1999), with economic power often interpreted as the key variable in the power balance within a marital relationship (Blumberg, and Tolbert Coleman, 1989). However the younger couples recruited to take part in this research all have double incomes, with both partners working full-time in professional occupations. As the female participants are not financially dependent on their partners one of the foundations of gender inequality has been removed from their relationships.

Research has indicated that the division of household resources within relationships is highly gendered, with many women failing to distinguish between personal and domestic savings (Wilson, 1987) and downplaying the value of their earnings in an effort to support their husbands' dominant position (Tichenor, 2005). The effort that goes in to managing a household budget has been grouped with other domestic chores; Safilios-Rothschild (1976: 339) distinguishes between 'orchestration power' and 'implementation power' in financial decision making. Within a relationship partners who hold the former have the power to make important and infrequent decisions that are particularly influential in determining their family's structure. Implementation power relates to the more time consuming task of managing relatively unimportant everyday financial decisions within the parameters set by the more dominant spouse.

Lewis (2001) notes that systems of household management have changed, with shifts in banking and female labour market participation undermining the power structures identified by research conducted in the 1970s and 80s. The younger couples here maintained relatively individual financial arrangements, with five out of the twelve couples having shared bank accounts with which to manage household expenses in addition to individual current and savings accounts. These couples all had joint mortgages on properties. The remaining seven couples maintained individual accounts but shared household expenses by taking responsibility for different direct debits. Most respondents explained that it was important to them to retain control of their own bank accounts:

'I think it's really important to have your own account, you know I don't want to have to justify spending eighty quid on a pair of shoes or whatever, I've earned that money.' (Christie, 5a)

'We don't have any secrets, but it's really important to have your own money I think, as an accountant I would never advise someone to give up their own account (laughs).' (Michelle, 8a)

'I would never give up my personal account and I'd never expect Carrie to either, I mean why would you, it would just cause arguments every time you wanted to spend your own money.' (John, 4b)

Retaining a sense of financial autonomy was important to respondents, with many referring to their 'own' money. This may be a way of negotiating the risk inherent in contemporary relationships, with participants seeing this as a way of protecting themselves in the eventuality that their relationships end. Where cohabiting couples share a mortgage they are still able to maintain a sense of financial independence:

'We are looking at properties, it's a risk but if it doesn't work out then you just sell the place and split it, no harm done.' (Jeff, 7b)

'We share a mortgage and have a joint account, but everything's fifty-fifty, and I suppose if we separated we'd just take out what we put in.' (Anna, 3a)

The older couples display a more traditional model, although most were reticent in discussions about finances. They all shared accounts, with one wife receiving an allowance from her husband, reflecting a particularly traditional style of money management (Pahl, 1989):

'I've got my own bank account and credit card, but that's for everyday, Trevor takes care of all the bills.' (Fiona, 21a)

One of the older female respondents explained how sharing finances was a symbol of commitment to the relationship:

'I don't understand that, when couples talk about "my money" and "his money", I mean are you together or what? Surely when you're married it's all the same pot and you both contribute in different ways? I don't understand how couples do that.' (Marie, 22a)

The younger respondents' fiscal independence from their partners could be interpreted as evidence of a shift towards more contingent relationships which are not expected to be permanent, although research has challenged the extent to which newly emerging individualized patterns of money management are indicative of greater gender equality overall (Vogler, Lyonette and Wiggins, 2008). It may be that this issue is forced upon younger couples, with traditional style of money management rendered obsolete by the dual-earner system. There are limitations from what we can infer from the operation of separate accounts (Lewis, 2001) and while finances appear to be kept separate, there is evidence that partners are happy to support their partners financially. Two respondents describe points in their relationships where one partner took financial responsibility for the other:

'When I finished my masters it took me about eighteen months to get a proper job, you know, like a salaried one, and for that time John covered the mortgage, he totally supported me and never complained. It's what you do when you're together, I'd do the same for him in a heartbeat.' (Carrie, 4a)

'Last year, Ben got made redundant, his company laid off half their staff and it was so scary I was the breadwinner. Luckily it was only for a couple of months until he started contracting, but that kind of thing really brings you closer together.' (Ali, 6a)

There has been a notable shift in the way that couples operate their finances which has been driven by the shift to dual-earner relationships. We should not overstate the significance of this development, which has to be placed in the context of other aspects of the social realities of heterosexual relationships. The arrival of children may also impact on this system (Lewis, 2001) at a future point in the participants' relationships. Yet it is significant that the economic power in the younger couples' relationships appears to be fairly well balanced. To unpick this further I also examined the significance that the respondents' attached to their careers.

Professional Status

A key aspect of change in heterosexual relationships is the trend towards both partners working. I purposely selected a sample of younger couples in which both partners were educated to at least degree level and enjoyed professional careers. The acronym 'DINKY', or 'double income no kids yet' has been coined to refer to such couples in recognition of the growing trend for professional couples to both work full time and defer having children (van Gils and Kraaykamp, 2008). With both partners working and no childcare to consider, the younger couples represented within this sample could potentially enjoy democratized relationships. However, the data indicates that although both partners participated in paid employment the man's job often took precedence in the accounts of both male and female respondents. While the women interviewed held professional positions, this is often played down in relation to their partners' careers. Equal power resources in an economic sense are undermined by the power processes at work within the heterosexual relationships studied.

Professional success is generally defined in terms of salary both male and female respondents, although this favours men as the gender pay gap for full-time workers in the UK is estimated at 9.1% in 2011 (Office for National Statistics, 2011b):

'I have a Masters, but he earns about double my salary, so I suppose his job's more important.' (Carrie, 4a)

'We met at work, he's not my boss or anything (laughs) but he is more senior, you know he earns more.' (Chloe, 9a)

'It's really difficult, I consider myself successful because I've played in New York, Barcelona, but because his work is more secure and he has a salary it's like his work is more important.' (Teresa, 12a)

Salary alone is not the sole reason for one partner's job taking precedence, as several of the women interviewed describe prioritizing their relationships over their careers:

'Because we do work for the same company I'm careful not to, er, step on his toes, I wouldn't sacrifice what we have for work it's just not worth it.' (Chloe, 9a)

'If it was like a work thing, like a good job abroad, I'd choose him over the job'. (Jane, 1a)

While a number of the women interviewed intimated that their relationships were more important than their careers, this can be contrasted by one of the male respondent's assertion that he would choose a promotion over his relationship:

'If I got a really good job offer abroad, I'd probably take it, my career's really important, and you have to make sacrifices sometimes.' (Jeff, 7b)

Another couple, Phil and Emma explain why they are moving to Australia for Phil's job:

'We are thinking of moving to Australia, as I've had a good offer, which will increase my salary.'

Would you move for Emma's job?
'Well (pause), I don't think she could earn as much, she works for the NHS.' (Phil, 11b)

'We're probably going to move out to Australia, because Phil's been offered a really good job.'

What about your job?
'I'll give it up, and hopefully find something when I get there. It's not as important really, as long as he's working.' (Emma, 11a)

There are structural issues downgrading the importance of the women's jobs, for example the fact that women generally earn less, work shorter hours and are expected to leave work to raise children. Statistical evidence indicating that women in their twenties out-earn men of the same age (Office for National Statistics, 2011b) has received much media attention, however this trend is reversed once workers approach their thirties. One female respondent, Anna, explains how this affects her colleagues' career choices in the medical profession:

> 'You see so many more female house officers going in to general practice than male, because you know as a GP you're going to have better working hours which matters if you're a woman who wants a family.' (Anna, 2a)

While women may still be expected to put their families and relationships ahead of their careers, the opposite is often demanded of men as the following quote illustrates:

> 'We do paternity leave, but there aren't any blokes that would do it, it would damage your career.'

> *Why's that?*
> 'It's just not done in my company.' (Jeff, 7b) (Employed by a major accountancy firm)

These factors are rarely challenged, rather they are accepted as justification for prioritizing the male partners' career within the relationships studied. It is interesting to note that Jeff refers to his company as 'we', suggesting an intimacy at least at the level of a personal relationship. Masculine identity is strongly linked to employment status (Connell, 1995), whereas women may be defined by other things such as their relationships, which is perhaps why they are more prepared to compromise. My respondents frequently used the longer hours worked by men, and the stress of their jobs as a reason for the lack of male participation in household chores:

> 'But my job's more stressful.' (Mark, 8b)

> 'But his job's more stressful than mine.' (Anna, 3a) (Both she and Carl are doctors, earning the same salaries)

> 'Well, she'd be at home more because I work longer hours, but I do the shopping sometimes and the odd bit of hoovering. If she worked as long hours as me then it wouldn't be fair.' (John, 4b)

'Work is my priority, which is why I'm a director now. I think that's fair enough, as I am young.' (Sam, 2b)

'My career's really important, and you have to make sacrifices sometimes.' (Jeff, 7b)

I would argue that the differences in male and female work pressures may be constructed by the couples interviewed in order to support and justify the inequalities within their relationships. The interviewees' responses reflect the findings of Mansfield and Collard's (1988) study of newly-wed couples. They found that both spouses down-played the value of the wife's job, using as justification women's lower earning power. The wives interviewed also viewed their paid work as secondary to looking after their homes and family (Mansfield and Collard, 1988: 155). While the younger women interviewed here do regard their careers as important, most of them indicate that their relationships take priority. Feminism is also viewed with suspicion by the younger women, which is perhaps one reason why they are unwilling to challenge inequalities:

'I definitely believe in equality, but I'm not some man-hating feminist.' (Jane, 1a)

To be defined as a feminist may be viewed by Jane as losing her feminine qualities (Dallos and Dallos, 1997: 124). There is also a suggestion that heterosexuality and feminism are mutually exclusive, perhaps because of the radical feminist attack on heterosexuality in the 1970s. Although the younger women have entered the traditionally masculine environment of the workplace, they are anxious not to compromise their femininity, and reflect Connell's description of 'emphasised femininity' (1987: 187) which is compliant with male power through displays of sociability rather than competence and the acceptance of marriage and childcare as a response to gender inequality within the workplace.

My findings also strongly support Evans' (2003) argument that women have achieved integration, rather than emancipation. Evans (2003: 45) cites Orwell's *1984*, in which 'real' power is held by men, although women are allowed into work and into apparent forms of sexual/public emancipation. It could be argued that women have not been liberated from patriarchy, rather they have been permitted to enter the workplace on men's terms, as they continue to be paid less, are expected to leave work to have children and see the areas of work that they enter in large numbers, such as teaching, downgraded in terms of status and pay. Within public contexts men and women are not equal, and rather than being challenged within intimate relationships this inequality is upheld.

Although several of the older women interviewed have worked, their husbands' careers were given priority, and the reason usually cited for this was that they were unable to earn as much money or achieve equal status; however one respondent, Marie, describes how she declined the offer of a promotion:

'I worked as a waitress, in an exclusive restaurant, but I just did it for pocket money, and to get out, really. I was offered the job of manageress several times, but that wasn't what I was interested in, I didn't want a career'. (Marie, 22a)

Marie describes her wage as 'pocket money', as if it was not important to her family, thus promoting the male breadwinner discourse. Two other older respondents describe their decision to choose raising their families over paid employment:

'I had a good job, for the council, but there was never really any question of Patrick staying at home to bring up the girls, you know, back then being a father meant providing for your family, and being a good mother meant that you had to look after your family. I never had any regrets about staying home and I didn't go back to work until Laura, my youngest, was in grammar school. But now we both work, and Laura starts at York University in September, so it's like I have more independence now.' (Anne, 23a)

'If I had stayed at the airport I'd be doing really well now, but I just wanted to stay at home with the boys.' (Fiona, 21a)

However, equality appears to be less of an issue for the older respondents, as power is openly divided along traditionally gendered lines; women have control over domestic matters, while their husbands are in charge of finances in the manner of Willmott and Young's 'symmetrical family' (1975), in which each spouse has a clearly defined role based on their gender. This ideal draws on the earlier model of the 'companionate marriage' (Finch and Summerfield, 1999), a post-war ideology of family based heterosexuality designed to stabilize and consolidate family life. Partnership and equality were emphasized, but in this context meant the teamwork of matched but strictly demarcated roles. The general consensus among the older respondents is that this is fair and justified by the perceived biological differences between the genders. This is in contrast to the younger couples, many of whom maintain a façade of equality while attempting to disguise or justify more complex power processes. Lewis (2001) suggests that there is less conflict within traditional relationships because there is little for partners to negotiate. The influence of the 'equals but different' (Dallos and Dallos, 1997: 116) discourse is evident here, as the older couples tended to see their relationships in terms of each spouse having different power bases that are equally influential, meaning that the marriage is balanced in terms of power. This discourse rests on ideas about different areas of expertise and complementarity, which stem from essentialist understandings of gender:

> 'But she has a lot of influence, she decided when we were going to have children, I just take care of the bills (laughs).' (Patrick, 23a)

> 'I think it's fair, I like it this way because he runs the business, but I'm in charge of the house, you know, how it's decorated, what we're eating, things like that.' (Fiona, 21a)

> 'Fiona organizes the house, and I do actually give her a salary for that out of the business, so she has her own pocket money. But I make all the big decisions, the business, and money.' (Trevor, 21b)

While Fiona and Trevor both express satisfaction with their division of labour, Trevor describes the allowance he gives her as 'pocket money' which is infantilizing rather than a recognition of the equal value of her labour. The older cohort of respondents frequently refer to essentialist gender stereotypes as justification for their respective roles:

> 'Men are more rational, though aren't they? If I made decisions, I'd do it because of feelings, I'm more emotional. He's so strong, he just says "let me take care of it", because he knows what a worrier I am.' (Marie, 22a)

The male breadwinner discourse strongly underpins the older respondents' discussions of employment, as it is assumed that the husband should be the major earner. Where wives do work this is downplayed as a minor income secondary to their role of wife and mother, which replicates findings of a previous study in which wives' incomes were underestimated and referred to as 'extras' (Mansfield and Collard's, 1988: 156). The younger couples' prioritization of the male partners' career is reminiscent of this, although both partners are expected to work full time. Lewis (2001) expresses scepticism at the view that women are now economically independent within relationships. She notes that, when children are involved, the 'one-and-a-half-breadwinner model' (Lewis, 2001: 17) has become the dominant pattern, as women work part-time in order to incorporate childcare, while the male partner continues with his career. As the younger couples interviewed here are childless this pattern is not apparent, however when discussed in the interviews the general expectation appeared to be that the female partner would be largely responsible for childcare in the future.

The assumption that dual-earner couples have achieved gender equality is displayed by the younger couples interviewed here and it is apparent that the employment status of women is used to gloss over myriad other inequalities inherent in dyadic heterosexual relationships. England (2010) maintains that women have had powerful economic incentives to move into the traditionally male domain of paid employment, however, while the devaluation of characteristics and activities associated with women persists, traditionally female activities hold little attraction for men. The asymmetry of this shift in gender roles has undermined changes in heterosexual couple relationships (England, 2010: 156).

While the younger female participants could be argued to have achieved near-equality within the workplace, this interpretation fails to acknowledge the discourses which continue to uphold men's work as more important. The older women interviewed have not attempted to attain equality through paid employment, but have largely focused on the traditionally feminine roles of being a wife and mother. While claiming that they have achieved equality based on difference is problematic, I would argue that they are not necessarily at a disadvantage compared to the younger generation, which has failed to acknowledge the importance of women's work within the home. The evidence here indicates that gender equality within the workplace has not resulted in automatic equality within heterosexual relationships; rather it operates to disguise the continuing inequalities upon which heterosexuality is based.

Summary

In this chapter the notions of power, equality and democracy within the context of heterosexual relationships have been explored in the context of finances and paid employment. The older generation of respondents tended to regard their traditional gender roles as complementary. While the home affairs are managed by the wife, the husband is the provider. Here, the male breadwinner discourse encourages older female respondents to down play their own experiences of employment outside of the house as secondary to their domestic work.

The younger generation discussed their experiences in very different terms, as both partners participate in full-time paid employment. While the younger women interviewed enjoy greater economic independence than the older female respondents, it is evident that their professional careers are not considered by either gender to be as important as their partner's. Empirical evidence (Gregson and Lowe, 1994) has challenged the assumption that women's increasing economic power inevitably leads to more egalitarian forms of domestic labour. The research findings presented here support the interpretation that greater gender equality in the workplace has not automatically resulted in the democratization of heterosexual relationships. Both male and female respondents support and justify the asymmetrical power structures within their relationships, rather than working to undermine them. References to structural inequality, such as greater pay and limited paternity leave for men, are employed by interviewees as an explanation for the power imbalances within their relationships, but are accepted rather than challenged. The male breadwinner discourse would at first glance appear to be obsolete for the younger generation, however the prioritization of the male partner's career, together with the widespread expectation that women will be the ones to stay at home to raise children, suggests the influence of this discourse in shaping my respondents' experiences and expectations. Ribbens McCarthy, Edwards and Gillies (2003) have noted that with regard to family life, individuals are continuing to draw on models popular in the 1970s, a finding that is reflected here. However, I reject the widely publicized view of Hakim (2009) who maintains that attempts to ensure gender equality in the workplace are misguided as the majority of women would rather stay at home, and instead argue that while personal relationships remain unequal women will always be disadvantaged in their careers.

Women also appear to have more invested in their relationships, as they are eager for further commitment and willing to put their partners first. Being in a relationship is important for the identity of both generations of female respondents in the same way that having a career validates the masculine identity of the men interviewed. While this imbalance continues, I would argue that heterosexual relationships will never become truly democratic. The next chapter shifts to a discussion of unpaid labour with an analysis of the gendered division of household work within the participants' relationships.

Chapter 4
Justifying Inequality: Explaining the Division of Housework

There exists a large body of sociological research on the gendered division of household labour, particularly in the context of increasing female participation in paid work. Yet for the couples interviewed here housework and cooking form a major part of their experiences within their relationships and garnered much discussion in both the interviews and focus groups (particularly from the female respondents). Rather than attempting to quantify the hours spent by each partner on domestic chores, the focus is on the explanations and justifications offered for the current division of labour by the respondents, and their feelings about this. Again, my concern is on the ways in which people construct the everyday meanings of their relationships (Harris, 2006) rather than in attempting to provide an objectively accurate description of those relationships (also see van Hooff, 2011).

The older couples interviewed openly admit to a separation of tasks along traditionally gendered lines. For the older women interviewed, looking after their families and homes takes priority over any paid work in which they may have engaged, as being a 'wife' is their primary role. For the younger generation, however, this justification does not exist. While the female partners take primary responsibility for the housework, excuses such as the male partner working longer hours or not being as skilled at cleaning, are utilized. An exception to this is food preparation, which many of the younger male respondents claimed to take responsibility for. However, cooking is framed in different terms to cleaning, with participants describing it as a creative outlet in contrast to the drudgery of cleaning.

The division of household tasks appears to form an important part of the narrative of my respondents' relationships possibly because it is one of the more tangible aspects of living with a partner, however it is only one 'story' of a relationship. Lewis (2001: 147) cautions against overstating the conclusions we can draw about a couple's relationship based on their division of housework, and I have tried to avoid extrapolating findings from this area onto other areas of my respondents' partnerships. However, the reasons given to explain the largely inegalitarian divisions of domestic labour exhibited by the men and women interviewed were related to other aspects of their lives, such as their paid employment.

The Division of Domestic Labour in Sociological Research

Research has consistently shown that women's increasing participation in paid employment has not been matched by men's participation in housework. Studies exploring the amount of time spent on domestic chores (including Hoschild, 1989; Presser, 1994; Gregson and Lowe, 1994; Birch, Le and Miller, 2009) continue to document the inegalitarian division of household labour within heterosexual relationships, with women undertaking around 70 per cent of the work (Mansfield and Collard, 1988; Baxter, 2000).

While a number of researchers (Nichols and Metzen, 1982; Pahl, 1984; Coltrane, 2000; Sullivan, 2000, 2004), provide evidence of a gradual increase in men's participation in domestic labour where their wives are working, the extra work done by husbands is comparatively insignificant measured against the extra work taken on by women, leading to the suggestion that women endure a 'double burden' (Jamieson, 1998), or 'second shift' (Hoschild, 1989) of housework and paid employment. While theorists such as Giddens (1991, 1992, 1999) and Beck and Beck-Gernsheim (1994, 1995, 2002) assert the demise of traditional gender roles and the emergence of a 'pure relationship' (Giddens, 1992), based on gender equality, the domestic division of labour between men and women has remained remarkably stable (Baxter, 2000), which is arguably more note-worthy than the minor increases in male contributions on this front.

Gregson and Lowe (1994) posit that within dual income households there is no automatic modification of the gendered division of household labour which has remained largely independent from male and female waged labour. Indeed, Arber and Ginn (1995) maintain that work and the family are autonomous spheres, with women's advances in employment rarely translating into advances in women's position within the family. In contrast to Sullivan's (2000) evaluation of quantitative data which would appear to indicate a more equitable division of domestic labour within middle class households, Gregson and Lowe (1994) also insist that social class is of minimal importance, as middle class couples are no more egalitarian than working class couples.

More recently, research has begun to focus on the reasons for this lack of change, and the methods used by couples to explain their divisions of domestic labour. Jamieson's analysis has led her to suggest that within heterosexual relationships, 'creative energy is deployed in disguising inequality, not in undermining it' (Jamieson 1999: 485). Bittman and Lovejoy (1993) maintain that within heterosexual partnerships couples defend an unequal division of labour as practical or temporary, rather than seeking to challenge it. Research conducted by Brannen and Moss (1991) found that working wives condone or misreport their husband's inadequate sharing of household chores and in doing so create a 'false consciousness', or what Hoschild (1989: 57) terms a 'cover story'. Similarly, Lewis (2001) argues that in the face of new found expectations of greater equality heterosexual couples have had to find ways in which to 'gloss the fact that much has stayed the same, particularly on the domestic front' (Lewis, 2001: 69). While the assumption that domestic work is automatically women's work is no longer acceptable within certain sociocultural groups, 'the same gender expectations persist in more complex forms, couched in terms of individual choices, standards and preferences' (Beagan et al., 2008: 668).

In analysing my respondents' accounts I am less concerned with the actual time and effort spent on housework than on their perceptions of the amount of work that they do compared with their partners, and how this is reconciled with discourses of equality. Before focusing on the explanations offered by the couples for their divisions of domestic labour, I briefly detail their accounts of how housework is shared.

Younger Couples' Division of Housework

My conversations with the younger respondents about the gendered division of domestic labour in their relationships provided little evidence to suggest that heterosexual relationships are becoming increasingly egalitarian, on this front at least. Although all of the female respondents were in full time employment, the majority of them also take often reluctant responsibility for housework. During the interviews, I directly questioned each respondent on the division of housework in their relationship and only one couple claimed to share domestic chores equally, with all others acknowledging that the female partner took on a greater share of the work. While partners interviewed separately inevitably give different accounts (Mansfield and Collard, 1988), generally couples' accounts matched fairly accurately when describing the amount of housework that they carried out. However, where responses did diverge was in their reactions to this. Many of the women interviewed expressed frustration at the amount of housework they felt they were expected to do:

'Housework, I do everything, then I have a raging fit and start shouting at Ian, then he'll do something, but it's because he doesn't realize something needs doing.' (Jane, 1a)

'It's kind of ended up that I do the cleaning and shit, and I don't know how it happened, but it's like two years later I'm a 1950s housewife or something.' (Ali, 6a)

Others appeared resigned to the fact that they were established as the partner responsible for the cleaning and did not seem willing to challenge this:

'I do it. It's not something that we've ever discussed, I just sort of have done it, and neither of us is sort of bold enough to bring it up now, so instead I just do it.' (Anna, 3a)

'I don't think it was really a decision, but I am the cleaner in the relationship, just because I'm better at it.' (Chloe, 9a)

'I do all of it. He is just so useless at cleaning, I mean he lived on his own for 10 years before we got together, and you think he'd be independent, but even then he was taking his washing round to his mum's, and she came round to clean.' (Sara, 10a)

'I'd say it was split about 70:30, I do most of the basic stuff, you know, polishing, cleaning the bathroom and kitchen, defrosting the fridge, and the oven, as I don't think he even knows that these things need doing.' (Teresa, 12a)

The majority of male respondents who admitted to carrying out less than half of the household chores expressed guilt, or offered explanations for this. In common with the newly married husbands interviewed in Mansfield and Collards' (1988: 121) study, merely questioning them on the division of labour was often interpreted as a criticism:

'Well (pause) I suppose Jane would do most of it, really. But I do cook. She'd say she did it all, but I do some stuff. I Hoover now, because we've got this really cool Dyson, so I do that sometimes.' (Ian, 1b)

'Ali would do most of it. We argue about it quite a lot. It's not fair, really, I should do more.' (Ben, 6b)

'Well, I would clean, but by the time I get there Chloe's already done it.' (Paul, 9b)

'Sara does do most of it, I've got to admit, but it's not because I think she should do it because she's a woman, it's just because she's got higher standards of cleanliness than me (laughs).' (Steven, 10b)

'I would never expect Teresa to do it because she's female, I think it's more down to personality, she's a clean freak and I'm not bothered by mess as much.' (Alex, 12b)

While ideals of equality do seem to be influential, in regard to housework this is something that the participants rarely achieve. Ben concedes that his level of participation in household chores is 'not fair', while Alex explains that they would 'never expect' his partner to do the cleaning because of her gender, however this does not appear to be enough to motivate them into taking on a larger or equal share. This was echoed in the focus group held with the younger men:

> *Do you do the cleaning?*
> S – Erm.
> *Group laughter*
> S – Basically she does, but it's only because I'm lazy, I really didn't expect her to do it because she was a woman.
> C – I must admit I do have to be told.
> P – I don't think I'm a normal lad like that because I'm quite tidy. As long as I don't start sitting down to take a piss.
> *(Male focus group, 20–35)*

The one participant who does admit to tidying is aware that this may compromise his masculinity. Joking 'as long as I don't start sitting down to take a piss', suggests that cleaning remains a highly feminized task, and that his cleanliness means that he is not a 'normal lad'.

There is further evidence that household tasks are allocated according to traditional gender roles, with men being expected to take primary responsibility for repairs and DIY:

> 'He expects me to clean, and I expect him to do certain things, like drill. But there's a crossover as well, like I look after the cars, because he's irresponsible and would never book an MOT.' (Jane, 1a)

> 'I do stuff on the house, though, like I put shelves up last week, and I sort the computer out.' (Carl, 3b)

> 'I do the repairs and building, so it's fair, really.' (Mark, 8b)

While the younger men and women ascribe to an ideology of equality, in practice the roles within their relationships are highly specialized according to gender. The inegalitarian division of household tasks is defended as practical because of the male partner's longer working hours or general lack of domestic skill, however, the end result is that the younger women have to take responsibility for both the unpaid labour of housework, and their paid careers. This apparent gap between the lived realities (according to the accounts given in the interviews) and ideals and expectations of the younger couples' relationships is the focus of this chapter, which seeks to explore the way the couples explain and justify this, both to themselves and to me, the interviewer.

'But he works longer hours': Respondents' Explanations for Inequalities

With only one couple in my sample claiming to divide domestic chores equally in the face of increasing expectations of equality, the reasons given for the divisions of domestic labour in the other eleven couple's relationships are explored here. It is argued that a number of common strategies are employed to reconcile this apparent gap between ideal and reality, which allow the couples to avoid admitting that their relationships fall short of the egalitarian ideal.

The first of these strategies is identified as competence. While none of the participants said that they felt that women should do the housework because of their gender, they used explanations that women are 'better at it', or have higher standards. McMahon (1999: 158) maintains that women's exacting standards of cleanliness are frequently used by men as a justification for their failure to undertake an equal share of the housework, and the men interviewed here described themselves as less able to do housework, or as having lower standards than their partners:

'It's not fair that she cleans up after my shit, so I do feel bad, and I do try to do some stuff, but then quite often she'll take over, because I'm not doing it right, or whatever.' (Alex, 12b)

'I don't expect her to do it, or anything, but for me to be bothered to do something, it has to be really filthy, and she'd never let it get that bad.' (Ben, 6b)

'I don't mind doing that stuff, but I think she's just a tidier person than me.' (Paul, 9b)

Female interviewees acknowledged that their high standards meant having to complete the housework themselves, and many used their partner's incompetence as a reason for the inequality within their relationships:

'I am the cleaner in the relationship, just because I'm better at it.' (Chloe, 9a)

'I do most of the basic stuff, you know, polishing, cleaning the bathroom and kitchen, defrosting the fridge, and the oven, as I don't think he even knows that these things need doing.' (Teresa, 12a)

'Because John's so bad at it, you know, he'll put things on the wrong wash or whatever, so I take over because it's quicker.' (Carrie, 4a)

The theme of male incompetence was also joked about in the focus group held with the younger women, in terms that it is assumed that the other participants and facilitator will share:

Is housework an issue?
C – Definitely, I would say it was one of our main sources of arguments, not serious but sort of everyday niggles when I'm trying to get him to do something and he thinks I'm nagging
J – Sometimes it's just easier to do it yourself, the housework, than fight about it, especially when men are so useless at cleaning, some are anyway
S – God there's a big difference between 'boy-clean' and 'girl-clean', half the time I have to redo it anyway (group laughter)
(Female focus group, 20–35)

Mansfield and Collard (1988) describe this as 'female chauvinism', and here it can be seen as a way for women to explain the amount of housework they do. Other research (Beagan et al., 2008) has described women's exacting standards as one of the main reasons that they end up doing more cooking, as well as cleaning. The distinction made in the focus group between 'boy-clean' and 'girl-clean' illustrates this popular idea that men and women's' different standards are innate and as a consequence cannot be challenged or overcome.

For some of the women interviewed, housework appears to be something that gives them a sense of satisfaction, which is the second justification employed by participants. Anna explained that being solely responsible for both cooking and cleaning made her feel 'independent and in control'. While this would initially seem contradictory it is possible that her home, as opposed to her workplace (Anna is a surgeon in a male-dominated field of medicine), could be seen as her territory. As many of the female respondents appear to have the primary responsibility for housework, this casts their male partners in a supplementary role. McMahon (1999: 6) argues that being cast as 'helpers' in the domestic sphere is a way for men to avoid taking on an equal share of the work.

The demands of paid employment were the third justification used in the interviews to explain the differences in amount of time spent on housework by partners. Female respondents, in particular, argued that the longer hours worked by their partners and higher levels of stress that they experienced meant that they could not be expected to undertake as many household chores.

'It is true that my job, as a probation officer, doesn't involve the same kind of hours, so I have more time for the house.' (Kate, 2a)

'His job is a lot more demanding, I suppose.' (Michelle, 8a)

'Well, I do most of the housework, but that's because he works longer hours than me.' (Emma, 11a)

'She'd be at home more because I work longer hours, but I do the shopping sometimes and the odd bit of hoovering. If she worked as long hours as me then it wouldn't be fair.' (John, 4b)

Respondents also emphasized the stress of the male partners' jobs as a justification for the lack of male participation in household chores:

'But my job's more stressful.' (Mark, 8b)

'But his job's more stressful than mine.' (Anna, 3a) (Both she and Carl are surgeons, earning the same salaries)

The longer hours frequently worked by a number of the male respondents enables the couples to justify the lack of male participation in household chores for practical reasons, which they cannot help. Vague references to the 'stress' and 'demands' of some of the male partners' careers are also employed in this way, with stress seemingly associated with salary and hours worked, rather than emotional labour. None of the female respondents claim to have stressful or demanding jobs. As explored in chapter three the research also indicated that although both partners worked, the man's job often took precedence, which may be why they dedicated more time to their careers. While the women interviewed enjoyed professional status at work this is played down in relation to their partners' careers, with the male-breadwinner ideology appearing to retain some influence over these dual-career couples. One female respondent explains that she chooses not to work late because of what she regards as her domestic responsibilities:

'If I work late, then the cleaning and the cooking doesn't get done, so even though it might cost me a promotion or whatever, I don't have the choice.'

But you said that John frequently works late.
'Yeah, but he doesn't have to make that choice, when he gets home everything's done.' (Carrie, 4a)

74

Although the male partners' longer working hours and the stress that is seen to accompany this are employed as a justification for the division of domestic tasks along traditional lines, it could be argued that in many cases women's domestic responsibilities prevent them from investing the same time and energy into their careers. These findings support Arber and Ginn's (1995) assertion that work and the family operate as autonomous spheres, with apparent advances in the position of women in the labour market failing to translate into commensurate advances in their relative positions within the family. The world of work has long been associated with gender inequality, and paid employment remains highly gendered with women and men seen as suited for different activities, men disproportionately represented in the top posts, and an enduring gender pay gap (Bradley 2007: 92). Within this context the male partners are more likely to be employed in higher paid positions with more prospect of advancement. Using this as a justification for an asymmetrical division of household chores not only undermines equality in the household, but also bolsters inequity in the workplace.

I would argue that the differences in male and female work pressures may be emphasized or constructed by the couples interviewed in order to support and justify the inequalities within their relationships. This is supported by McMahon, who maintains that where men occupy privileged positions in the labour market with accompanying demands on time and energy, this is viewed as a constraint to equality within the domestic sphere (1999: 172). While the younger women interviewed here do regard their careers as important, most of them indicate that their relationships take priority.

The fourth strategy used to justify an asymmetrical distribution of household chores was identified as a division between housework and food preparation. While the majority of male respondents left the bulk of cleaning to their partners, six claimed to take primary responsibility for cooking, which could traditionally be seen as a female task, and takes up more time than any other single household chore (Kemmer, 2000). However, this appears to be a different experience to housework, as the men do it because they gain pleasure from it:

'And I really like doing it, I like creating recipes, it's something I'm really in to.' (Ian, 1b)

'I do the cooking. Christie makes food, but I wouldn't call it cooking, more like bunging something in the microwave. I love making really gorgeous, complicated recipes.' (Niall, 5b)

'As for the cooking, I do a lot of that, I've got lots of recipe books and things, all the men in my family do the cooking, we're better at it. My dream is to open my own restaurant.' (Paul, 9b)

'But I make the tea, which I think is a pretty big thing, because I love cooking and I'm much better at it than she is (laughs). Don't tell her I said that, she'll kill me.' (Steven, 10b)

These men talk about cooking in very different terms than are used by the women to discuss cleaning. Women talk about housework as a chore that needs to be done, not something that is interesting or enjoyable. The creativity involved in preparing elaborate meals makes cooking more appealing than cleaning, and it is also something that garners praise, unlike cleaning. With female partners spending more time on other household chores, the time spent on complicated recipes may not be available to them in the same way that it is to male respondents. Foodwork is also recognized in its own right, rather than as part of a bundle of general household tasks (Kemmer, 2000) and the popularity of male celebrity chefs has worked to frame cooking as a form of creative leisure (Swenson, 2009). Men appear to have more power in the relationship to decide whether to cook or not, as it is a choice they make, whereas women do not appear to have the same luxury. However, the increase in younger men taking responsibility for cooking does represent a significant shift. Debbie Kemmer's (2000) qualitative research into a sample of dual-earner, childless heterosexual couples in Edinburgh and Glasgow also found that women were exclusively responsible for cooking in only half of the couples she interviewed. She concluded that while a rigid gendering of roles was not apparent in her sample, in most households women continue to carry the burden of responsibility, combined with full-time paid employment. With regard to the younger couples here, while food preparation is no longer viewed as an exclusively feminine task and may be a source of pride for the male respondents, the bulk of the more onerous household tasks have remained the responsibility of the female partner.

Having discussed the strategies employed by my respondents to justify inegalitarian divisions of household labour, in the next section I focus briefly on the situation of the one couple who claim to share tasks equally.

The Anomaly of Equality

With only one couple out of the twelve interviewed claiming to have achieved total equality with regard to household chores, here I explore how this has been achieved. Dawn describes the division of labour as 'very simple, and very equal' and Jeff explained further:

> 'We share it, I probably do most of the cooking, because I have more time, her work takes her out quite a lot more, other than that we do share it. It's probably fifty-fifty to be fair. She does more of the washing, because she's more bothered by it than I am. You know, I've lived on my own for five years. We also split the bills. Everything is fifty-fifty split.' (Jeff, 7b)

Dawn and Jeff are the only couple who claim to share the housework equally. As a result of the long hours they both work (as accountants at the same firm), housework is done by whoever has more time. This appears to have been a conscious effort by the couple, fully endorsed by Jeff, which is perhaps the major difference in this relationship, as without his cooperation it is quite likely that Dawn would have to take care of the chores, as with the other couples interviewed. However, it is also worth noting that of all the respondents, Dawn and Jeff had been together for the least amount of time (nine months) and although they did live together at the time of the interviews, Dawn had temporarily moved into Jeff's shared flat until their new house was ready. When this happens Jeff may feel less responsible for the housework, as Dawn explains 'At the moment Jeff does most of it, because he feels it's his house'.

Furthermore, Jeff makes it clear further into the interview that his priority is his career and that he would expect Dawn to relinquish her job in order to raise any children they may go on to have. It would appear that, as VanEvery (1996) has observed, women are dependent on men's agreement for their ability to live in an anti-sexist way, as they rarely have the power resources to insist that their partners share the domestic work with them.

Although Dawn and Jeff were the only couple to claim to share tasks equally, another couple claim to have resolved the issue by employing a cleaner, which in effect removes the problem without fully resolving it:

> 'We decided to split it equally, but it just didn't happen, and then it was like 'sod it, we both earn good money, let's get a cleaner.' (Christie, 5a)

> 'Neither of us do the cleaning; we pay someone (laughs). Christ, it's worth it not to have Christie nagging me about washing, or whatever.' (Niall, 5b)

This technique is supported by Stacey's (1996) argument that the middle classes represent the minority who have the available resources to enjoy the potential of postmodern family options, for example, they have sufficient income to employ cleaners thus removing the issue of dividing household chores. Furthermore, Gregson and Lowe's (1994) research into the increase in waged domestic labour found that the employment of a cleaner did not normally bring about a more egalitarian division of domestic labour among heterosexual couples. In the majority of cases, men withdrew completely from domestic work, leaving chores to be shared between the women interviewed and their cleaners (Gregson and Lowe, 1994: 73).

Negotiation and the Division of Domestic Work

Giddens stresses the role of communication and negotiation in late modern relationships, however in many of the cases studied here, it is assumed that the female partner will take on the responsibility for cleaning the house without discussion. Where this issue was negotiated the female partner had to initiate the discussion, which placed her in the weaker position. Many of the female interviewees complain of frustration as their attempts at negotiation fail to achieve long-term change:

'Sometimes I try to negotiate, like 'we've got to sort this out, we've got to sort this out', but nothing ever happens.'(Jane, 1a)

'I had to ask him to do things again and again, as it would be ages before he'd get round to it, and then he'd call me a nag. I don't think it's very fair.' (Kate, 2a)

'Well, it's always me that starts it, then he gets defensive, and we end up fighting, so, no, I wouldn't say it's negotiated (Laughs).' (Ali, 6a)

Housework also becomes a major cause of conflict within relationships, as the women interviewed experience conflict within themselves, for taking responsibility for the housework (Kemmer, 2000) and with their partners:

'I'd make suggestions to Sam, and it would turn into an argument. He is adamant that he does clean, he does cook, but if you ask him when he last did something he'll just laugh, and think it's funny, whereas I don't think it's funny.' (Kate, 2a)

'I do everything, then I have a raging fit and start shouting at Ian.' (Jane, 1a)

'Cleaning is definitely the major cause of arguments. I get pissed off with doing it all, and then have a go at him, then he accuses me of nagging. We get over it, and then we'll have the same argument, like months later. So I don't suppose we ever solve, deal with it really.' (Carrie, 4a)

'I'd say that we definitely argue about that most, just because I think it needs doing, and he doesn't.' (Sara, 10a)

Feeling 'unappreciated' for the amount of housework they do is often more of a complaint for the female respondents than the work itself, as is illustrated by Anna's response:

'After a little while I start to think 'where's the appreciation for this, tell me more often thank you'. I don't really mind doing it; I just want it to be recognized.' (Anna, 3a)

Evidence from the interviews with the younger women suggests they use various strategies in order to even out the allocation of tasks, with varying degrees of success. The first technique is direct confrontation, which may begin as an attempt at negotiation, but often deteriorates into an argument:

'We do fall out about it quite a lot, like sometimes when I come home from work and the house is a tip, it really fucks me off, and we'll have a fight.' (Ali, 6a)

While this approach often achieves short term gains, there is little evidence to suggest that this is more than a token effort on behalf of the male partners:

'I'll have a go, but nothing ever really changes, so I don't mind generally, until I periodically lose it.' (Ali, 6a)

'We do fight over it, and then he'll do it for like a day, before he reverts into his old self.' (Carrie, 4a)

'Sometimes I try to negotiate, like 'we've got to sort this out, we've got to sort this out', but nothing ever happens.' (Jane, 1a)

The second strategy is unspoken resistance, for example, going 'on strike':

'I occasionally go on strike, but he doesn't seem to notice, so I crack first.' (Sara, 10a)

'Sometimes I have little stubborn episodes where I stop doing laundry, and refuse to clean up, but I crack before he does. Sooner or later I think "sod it, I'm just going to have a much bigger pile to do in the end", so I just carry on.' (Anna, 3a)

By withholding their labour, these women hope that their partners will notice and increase their own contribution, however as a strategy it proves ineffective as the women in question describe how they 'crack' before anything changes. This strategy also undermines the importance of openness and communication within late modern relationships.

Although housework was a major cause of conflict for the younger couples, it was not rated as important enough to end the relationship over, and perhaps because of this is rarely resolved. Interestingly, only female interviewees spoke of housework as the primary cause of arguments with their partners. When questioned further, one male respondent stated:

> 'Well, Jane gets all hyper about it, but I just humour her. It's not like we'd ever split up about something as, well, silly as who cleans the toilet (laughs).' (Ian, 1a)

Ian's dismissal of housework as important to his relationship illustrates the difference in his own and his partner's perspectives. He jokes about how something as inconsequential as housework would never end their relationship, whereas his partner, Jane, describes it as something that is extremely important to her. Negotiation appears to achieve little change, as any increases in the amount of domestic work carried out by the male respondents tail off. Within this context, female respondents are at a disadvantage, as while they may initially have taken care of the cleaning out of love for their partner it has become defined as their responsibility, as the following quote illustrates; 'I didn't mind at first, but now he has no idea how to clean, or change sheets, or pay bills' (Kate, 2a).

These findings echo Dempsey's (1998) Australian study of the negotiation process that goes into the gendered division of domestic labour. Interviews with sixty-six married women and sixty-two married men found that half of the women had attempted to get their husbands to share, or take responsibility for, 'inside' jobs such as cleaning and cooking. However, half of these women failed to achieve lasting gains, or made only token gains. I would argue that once a routine has been established within a relationship, renegotiating roles becomes more problematic, particularly when accompanied by the justifications made by both male and female respondents in defence of the gendered division of labour.

Older Couples' Division of Housework

For the older couples interviewed here, housework is generally divided along traditionally gender-stereotyped lines, with women taking primary responsibility for both housework and childcare and their husbands undertaking repairs and other masculine tasks, as well as taking financial responsibility for their family. Unlike the younger couples, the older couples interviewed all have children (who are no longer dependent), meaning that childcare is an issue that they will have had to address. For most of the older couples the division of domestic labour is rigidly gendered:

'Who does the housework? Do you really have to ask? Moi, that's who does it, moi (laughs). I'd collapse with shock if Trevor did any. I think it's fair, I like it this way because he runs the business.' (Fiona, 21a)

'I worked until we decided to have children, when I was about 26, then it seemed right, natural really, that I would be the one to stop working. I don't understand why you would work when you have young children, I mean why have them if you're going to pack them off to nursery at three months? And, of course with staying at home, you end up doing the housework, though I do think that it is really a woman's job.' (Marie, 22a)

'Even though it was the seventies, and we knew about feminism, no one would have married you if you weren't going to cook and clean, and raise children.' (Barbara, 25a)

'For my generation, women in their fifties now, you knew when you got married that you were going to have to stay at home to do the housework, and bring up the kids.' (Liz, 24a)

'I don't do much housework, but you know I work twelve hour days, and Fi hasn't worked for over twenty-five years, so that's her job. I think she gets a good deal, she doesn't have the boys to look after anymore, and she likes to clean.' (Trevor, 21b)

In discussing the division of housework both Trevor and Fiona argue that their relationship is fair, as Trevor is the breadwinner while Fiona is the homemaker. However, there is an underlying notion that Fiona is not as capable as Trevor, possibly because of her gender, as Trevor does not consider looking after the house as proper 'work'. This is revealed further into my interview with Trevor, when I ask him if he would have stayed at home to look after his two sons when they were children:

'Well, I wouldn't have minded, no. But I could never just do that, I would have done something else as well, I would have run a business from home, you could do that and look after children at the same time.' (Trevor, 21b)

While Trevor maintains that he would have happily taken responsibility for childcare, he is dismissive about the amount of time and effort involved in raising children and indicates that it is not a full-time job.

The general consensus among the older respondents is that, although housework and childcare is allocated to the women on account of their biology, this is fair as it complements the male role of breadwinner. Again, the influence of the 'equals but different' discourse is evident. In 1980, Edgell (cited in Lewis, 2001: 60) noted that the unequal division of paid and unpaid labour was the key issue in understanding the relationships of middle-class couples. For couples at the time, jointness was based on the unequal division of work. Interestingly, my respondents' initial dividing up of housework is not necessarily fixed, as where the husband has retired a certain amount of renegotiation may take place and tasks may be more equally shared, an event that shows fluidity of roles, even after thirty years of marriage, and the importance of the lifecourse in shaping experiences:

> 'Now we're both at home all day, Anton does more, I still do most of the housework, but now he does the hoovering, and cleans the windows, which helps. When he retired I got fed up with doing all the work, so I told him he had to help me more.' (Marie, 22a)

Marie and Anton are a couple who embraced more traditional roles earlier in their lives, yet have worked out a more egalitarian balance in retirement. Marital relationships are often a site of change at retirement (Barnes and Parry, 2003), as roles and relationships associated with individual's previous labour market positionings are transformed. Throughout the lifecourse, men and women inhabit a range of gendered identities (Barnes and Parry, 2003) and retirement may signal a decrease in role differentiation between married couples as they renegotiate a more equal division of domestic labour.

> 'Obviously, now he doesn't work anymore, we share cleaning and housework a lot more. I don't think he had any idea of the amount of work I had to do, the house was always clean by the time he came home.' (Liz, 24a)

Liz claims that her husband was simply not aware of the work involved in maintaining their house, which supports views of housework as an 'invisible' labour that only draws attention when it is not done. The older husbands' willingness to help out when asked is not reflected in the younger sample, and it is possible that the older couples have higher standards of cleanliness, or simply that after twenty-five years of marriage they have learnt to compromise.

While the older women interviewed do not complain about their own roles, the three with daughters are pleased that women now have more choices:

'Well, my daughter has a degree, and a career, so it wouldn't be fair then, for her to have to do all the cleaning and cooking wouldn't be fair, it would be like a different, another job.' (Marie, 22a)

'I think things are different now, you know because women work, they have careers, and they aren't interested in having families young, like we were, like my eldest says she doesn't want to get married and have children, and while she might change her mind it's good she has the choice, there isn't so much pressure now.' (Anne, 23a)

The older female respondents' perception of younger women's liberation from traditional roles is greater than the social reality indicated by empirical findings, which suggest that there remains pressure for women to find a male partner and take responsibility for housework and childcare. There is an assumption that because women are working full time, they do less housework, which this study and others have found little evidence to support.

Other older female respondents express some disapproval of the perceived lack of domestication of younger women:

'One of my sons lives with a career woman, and she's not interested in marriage, or cleaning, or anything. She doesn't even iron his shirts, so he still brings his washing home for me to do. I preferred it our way, we had a more old fashioned way.' (Fiona, 21a)

Fiona is unable to support any change in women's roles, possibly because she feels that her son is being neglected by his partner, the 'career woman'. Rather than taking on the chore of ironing, her son has merely passed it on to his mother, another woman.

'Women aren't satisfied with things like we were, they want to be like men, but one of you has to be the wife and mother, don't they? I know men can stay at home, but it doesn't seem right, I just can't take them seriously, what man would want to stay at home, while his wife provides for him?' (Barbara, 25a)

For Barbara, the roles of 'wife' and 'mother' remain highly feminized, as she regards any man choosing to stay at home with suspicion. Her strong feelings suggest an element of defensiveness with regard to her own choices.

Summary

The interviews conducted illustrate the gulf between the ideology of late modern relationships and experiences of couples, as well as the interplay between the two. While most of the younger couples felt they should in theory share domestic tasks equally, this happened in only one case. For all of the other couples, the responsibility for cleaning fell to the female partner, or was avoided by the employment of a cleaner. My findings show that the picture has remained largely in stasis since Gillis' (1985) study of young, heterosexual couples. He found that although the ideology in relationships is one of equality, this does not translate into practice, as with homeownership relationships become overwhelmed with stereotyped roles.

This study has produced little evidence to support Sullivan's (2000) assertion that couples within higher socio-economic groups, such as those interviewed here, have achieved a position of near-equality, as while my younger respondents verbally endorsed an equal split their everyday practices failed to live up to this. As Jane Lewis (2001) argues, there is remarkably little conflict between men and women over the fundamental inequalities represented by the division of household work, even though expectations as to the 'ought' have increased (Lewis, 2001: 67). She cites the 1993 British Social Attitudes Survey, which shows widespread support for the ideal of equality between the sexes although only a quarter of those surveyed believed this represented the reality of lived relationships. Having careers equal to their partners also appeared to have little effect on the amount of housework carried out by the women interviewed here.

The older couples were aware of the discourse of equality, but felt that it did not apply to them, as they had already established a gendered division of labour within their relationships. The respondents seemed satisfied with their roles, perhaps because as Lewis (2001) suggests, with traditional roles there is little room for negotiation. However, in the case of two of the older couples where the male partner had retired, their contribution did increase, although this was seen as an expression of care rather than an endorsement of gender equality. At retirement marital relationships may undergo changes, as couples renegotiate a more equal division of domestic labour (Barnes and Parry, 2003). Although the ideologies influencing the two generations differ, the actual division of chores practiced are remarkably similar.

Competence was a major reason cited for the allocation of tasks, echoing Mansfield and Collard's (1988) study where the experienced performer of a task was thought to be the natural candidate for that job, by which reasoning women were allocated traditionally feminine tasks such as cleaning while men engaged in DIY. Competence was used to justify male participation in cooking, as a number of the younger of the male respondents considered themselves more skilled in this area. The fact that so many of the younger men took responsibility for the cooking is significant, as for the older couples interviewed cooking continues to be viewed as an exclusively female role.

The relationship between heterosexuality and inequality in the division of household work is crucial, as heterosexuality remains an institution which encompasses more than just sex. Stevi Jackson (1996c: 35) argues that heterosexuality is founded as much on men's access to women's unpaid labour as to their bodies, something that is evident in the participants' relationships. Jo VanEvery's (1996: 41) study of anti-sexist living arrangements found that women are dependent on men's agreement for their ability to live in an anti-sexist way, which is played out here in the relationship of the one couple who enjoy an equal division of domestic labour, as it was initiated by the male partner.

The data presented here supports other empirical evidence that suggests that, with regard to domestic labour, dual-earner couples have not achieved equality. However, younger women do have financial independence, which raises the question as to why these women are prepared to stay in unequal relationships. Jamieson (1998, 1999) suggests that the fact that many relationships don't qualify as 'pure' doesn't mean that they are not intimate, as inequalities do not stop many couples from having loving relationships. Rather than gender roles being obsolete, the findings suggest that within many heterosexual relationships gender is everything. The findings presented in the following chapter focus on the role of sex in the participants' relationships.

Chapter 5
Freed from the Phallus?
Sex in Relationships

Sex is seen as a particularly important and unique element of couple relationships by theorists, popular culture and individuals alike. As such it is an area in which ideology and discourse are particularly relevant in informing the ways in which the participants construct and discuss their sex lives throughout the course of the interviews and focus groups. While older respondents focus on the sexual behaviour of young women today in comparison to the time of their own youth, the younger couples display a need to live up to the ideal of a fulfilling and exciting sex life within their own relationships. This chapter explores these issues, and reflects on how liberalized heterosexuality has actually become in the respondents' accounts. Following a review of the literature, and a consideration of methodological issues, the focus is on the younger couples, who were more open in discussions about sex within both the interviews and focus groups. I consider the importance they attach to sex to their relationships and the way that it is linked to issues of power and gender identity. As the older respondents preferred to discuss sexual behaviour in more general terms I explore this in the final section of the chapter, including an analysis of the ways that they contrasted the behaviour of their own generation in the 1970s and that of the current younger generation.

The Liberalization of (Hetero)Sexuality?

The ubiquity of sexual images and references within late modern society gives rise to the popular interpretation that western cultures are sexually liberated (Jackson and Scott, 2004). However, our supposed freedom coexists with the persistence of essentialist understandings of sex as a biologically driven act of individual intimacy which is somehow beyond the realm of the social and therefore sociological enquiry. Recent research and scholarship has done much to rectify this, although a focus on subversive and diverse sexual practices means that we still know little about 'everyday, mundane, conventional sexual lives' (Jackson, 2008: 34) particularly within heterosexual relationships.

The transformation of intimate relationships documented by Giddens, Beck and Beck-Gernsheim and other theorists is said to have been accompanied by changes in sexual identities, as sexuality has ceased to be a 'fixed terrain' (Hawkes, 1996: 106). The result is the predominance of 'plastic sexuality' (Giddens, 1992: 178), in which sex has been severed from reproduction and functions as a 'malleable feature of self' (Giddens, 1992: 15). The modern tendency to limit family size, followed by the availability of modern contraception and the introduction of new reproductive technologies, form the origins of plastic sexuality. Manifestations of plastic sexuality include the flourishing of homosexuality, the separation of female sexual pleasure from heterosexual intercourse, and the general replacement of 'perversion' with 'pluralism'; in short, plastic sexuality 'frees sexuality from the rule of the phallus' (Giddens, 1992: 2). Sexuality is an area of life in which individuals have to reflexively engage, as 'the 'biological justification' for heterosexuality as 'normal', it might be proposed, has fallen apart' (Giddens, 1992: 178–179). Giddens concedes that dualistic sex divisions remain in place, but predicts that 'as anatomy stops being destiny, sexual identity more and more becomes a lifestyle issue' (Giddens, 1992: 199). The idea that late modern social processes have radically transformed sexualities and personal relationships has been supported by other theorists (Weeks, 1995; Roseneil, 2000) as well as wider public discourse.

The liberalization of sexuality is often dated to the 1960s (Jackson and Scott, 2004), to be contrasted with the Victorian era as the height of sexual repression (Hawkes, 1996). Post World War II, sexuality moved to the centre of public debate, through student protests, counter-culture movements, the availability of the contraceptive pill and legalized abortions. In the late 1960s and 1970s, sexual liberation became central to anti-authoritarian and revolutionary movements. Giddens writes that the 'sexual revolution' involves two basic elements, firstly 'the revolution in female sexual autonomy', and secondly, 'the flourishing of homosexuality' (Giddens, 1992: 28). Giddens perceives these changes as 'irreversible', and profound in the consequences that they have had on late-modern sexuality.

It is undeniable that the 1960s ushered in far-reaching sexual reforms, including the availability of the contraceptive pill and the legalization of abortion (Segal, 1987: 75). These changes gave women control of their own fertility (although this had to be accessed through physicians) and severed the previously unassailable link between sex and reproduction. However, the liberation and celebration of female sexuality was 'a double-edged sword' (Hawkes, 1996: 108), as the recognition that women had sexual desires and feelings came with an obligation to exercise these desires through heterosexual sex. Hawkes notes that what may have offered true sexual autonomy and liberation to women was subordinated to a new construction of women's sexuality by men. Many women did enjoy the sexual freedom offered to them in the 1960s and 70s, and pursued Erica Jong's (1974) ideal of the *zipless fuck* throughout these decades, however, it became apparent to feminists that the sexual revolution had resulted in a male defined sexuality that continued to undermine women, a point that was illustrated by the growth in pornography (Segal, 1996: 79). This sexual 'liberation' was embodied by manuals such as *The Joy of Sex* by Comfort published in 1972, which on deeper analysis paid little attention to female sexual pleasure (Dallos and Dallos, 1997: 131). Similarly, in the 1960s and 70s, Masters and Johnson insisted that vaginal penetration was adequate stimulation to bring a woman to orgasm (Segal, 1987: 90). Hawkes notes behind the supposed modernism of their approach, Masters and Johnson followed a traditionally gendered approach, and prioritized heterosexuality over homosexuality. Their work contributed to the 'anxiety making' (Hawkes, 1996: 69) tradition in regard to sex, through the promotion of orgasm as the ultimate goal, which consequently pathologized women and men who were unable to achieve this through coitus.

By the mid-1970s second wave feminists made efforts to reclaim women's sexuality and turned their focus to the negative aspects of heterosexual relationships, with recognition that the personal was political (Millett, 1970). At this time Anne Koedt (1972/1996) published work stating that the penis was irrelevant to women's sexual pleasure as the clitoris was the main source of sexual arousal in women. Shere Hite's first study into female sexuality in 1976 revealed that while only a third of the women surveyed could orgasm easily through heterosexual intercourse, the majority of women were able to orgasm from clitoral or pubic area stimulation. In *The Female Eunuch* (1970), Germaine Greer argued that the sexual revolution was a fallacy in which women adopted the manners of their oppressors and practiced oppression on their own behalf. The work of Betty Friedan (1965) and Hannah Gavron (1966) contributed towards a recognition that married women and mothers had been forgotten in the 1960s and were unable to reconcile the gulf between their own lives and the ideals promoted at the time (Hawkes, 1996: 110–11).

Attention was also focussed on domestic violence (Segal, 1987: 82), and feminists became increasingly critical of heterosexuality, a rebellion that was enabled by women's increasing participation in the labour force and consequent independence from men. Segal, (1987: 93) notes that by the mid-1970s, heterosexual sex had been removed from the context of personal relations, and placed in terms of personal need. Campaigns centred around abortion, pornography and sexual violence had a challenge to patriarchal sexual relations at their core (Hawkes, 1996: 111). At this point, the belief that heterosexual feminists were 'traitors to the cause' (Jackson and Scott, 1996: 14) began to circulate, as theorists such as Sheila Jeffreys, Andrea Dworkin and in 1979, the Leeds Revolutionary Feminists, began to imply that heterosexuality and feminism were mutually exclusive. Dworkin argued that under patriarchy, heterosexual penetration is a form of occupation and colonialization and as such is always rape, which serves to symbolize men's hatred of women (cited in

Smart, 1996: 167). Women who continued to engage in heterosexual relations with men were therefore seen to be collaborating with them. Adrienne Rich went on to contest the assumption that most women are heterosexual, through her argument that heterosexuality is imposed upon women and is constantly reinforced by social constraints which serve to assure the male right of 'physical, economic and emotional access' (Rich, 1978/1996: 135). Rich concludes that the lesbian alternative has largely been rendered invisible as a further means of enforcement.

This turn in feminist thought made an important contribution to the study of sexualities through the identification of heterosexuality as socially, rather than biologically, constructed in order to serve the needs of patriarchy. However, these radical feminist claims have been challenged as problematic. Firstly, they portray women as the victims of male dominance. As Segal points out, if this were true, women would have to be 'blind and stupid' (Segal, 1987: 103) not to stop this. Segal's alternative is the construction of new images of women's active sexuality, as opposed to the portrayal of women as victims. It could also be argued that the maintenance of heterosexual relationships with men may have different meanings for women of different ethnic backgrounds (Kanneh, 1996: 172). While gender differences are reproduced through heterosexual relationships, this is not always inevitable, as every relation is 'a site of potential change as much as it is a site of reproduction' (Hollway, 1996: 99). Smart (1996: 165) expresses concern with the ways in which some feminists view heterosex as the defining element of female oppression. She argues that by doing this, radical feminists unintentionally bolster male power and privilege. Smart offers a more contextualized reading, in which there are multiple meanings attached to different sexualities at the same time. Through her writing, Smart deconstructs the 'mythic status of unitary, transhistorical heterosexuality', and writes of 'heterosexualities and the diverse and competing meanings associated with and deriving from these heterosexualities' (Smart, 1996: 166).

Second wave feminist thought has been further challenged by the 'Queer turn'. Butler (1990) pioneered a new way of looking at gender, which moves beyond the masculine/feminine binary to portray gender as fluid and unstable, as opposed to fixed and unchanging. Butler includes in her work a critique of contemporary feminism, which aims to represent women as a homogeneous group, with little allowance for social class, ethnicity, sexuality, and individual differences; 'the political assumption that there must be a universal basis for feminism, one which must be found in an identity assumed to exist cross-culturally, often accompanies the notion that the oppression of women has some singular form discernible in the universal or hegemonic structure of patriarchy or masculine domination' (Butler, 1990: 3). Butler argues that the effect of categorizing all women as a unified group standing in opposition to men has in reality run contrary to feminist aims, as describing the differences between women and men as fundamental and irreconcilable makes the achievement of true equality impossible. Butler is critical of radical feminist attempts to identify men as 'the enemy', which she argues 'uncritically mimics the strategy of the oppressor instead of offering a different set of terms' (Butler, 1990: 13).

Queer theory offers a deconstruction of the way that society views gender roles, in order that individual identity can be developed, as 'persons only become intelligible through becoming gendered' (Butler, 1990: 16). Gender identity is largely constructed through differentiation from the 'opposite sex', a formulation that maintains the binary masculine/feminine model, which consequently supports the naturalization of heterosexuality.

The popular view that there has been a repression of sexuality since the seventeenth century which was only challenged in the 1960s was also challenged by Foucault (1979). Foucault's critique of what he termed 'the repressive hypothesis' rests on three doubts that he had (Foucault, 1990: 10). He queried whether sexual repression is an established historical fact, whether power is exercised through the repression of sexuality, and if challenges to this repression contest the mechanisms of power, or form part of the same network. In short, Foucault questions whether there really was 'a historical rupture between the age of repression and the critical analysis of repression' (Foucault, 1990: 10). In fact, Foucault argues, the preoccupation with restricting and controlling sex, which has characterized our society since the seventeenth century, served to transform sex into a discourse for all. Making sexuality sinful did not eradicate it; rather it was reinforced and became ubiquitous. The question of sex became a constant preoccupation, and silence on the matter was part of this discourse.

Sex also became a 'police matter' (Foucault, 1990: 24) in the eighteenth century, as it was at the heart of economic and political analysis, for example in the case of the Victorian preoccupation with the problem of population. Sex and sexuality was also addressed by medicine, psychiatry and criminology, as well as sexology. The popular understanding of Victorian societies as prudish and repressive fails to acknowledge the omnipresence of discourses concerned with sexuality; 'in this time sex was forced out of hiding and constrained to lead a discursive existence' (Foucault, 1990: 33).

Having established the existence of a discourse on sexuality in our recent history Foucault turned his attention to our preoccupation with talking about sex today, and our belief and satisfaction that by doing so we are somehow 'defying established power' (Foucault, 1990: 6). There exists a certain irony in our society 'which has been loudly castigating itself for its hypocrisy for more than a century, which speaks verbosely of its own silence, takes great pains to relate in detail the things it does not say, denounces the powers it exercises, and promises to liberate itself from the very laws that have made it function' (Foucault, 1990: 8). In the late twentieth century discourse surrounding sexuality has shed much of the negativity associated with sexuality in the last century, however, Foucault's argument reveals that there is a persistence of some of the older themes, for example the interplay between sexuality and truth which was once played out through the confessional but has been replaced by, amongst other things, psychoanalysis. We now reside in a 'confessing society' (Foucault, 1990: 59) in which we are compelled to tell the truth, whose production is imbued with the relations of power. However, Foucault acknowledged that although discourse reinforces and transmits power, it also has the potential to undermine and expose it. A straightforward notion of repression is replaced in Foucault's work by a more complex mechanism for social regulation; power exists in many forms and permeates various discourses, and has become disciplinary, as opposed to sovereign.

Foucault's interpretation of disciplinary power and the ways in which sexuality continues to be regulated jar with Giddens' analysis of late modern relationships as almost entirely liberated and reflexive. In response, Giddens (1992: 24) critiques Foucault for his overemphasis of sexuality at the expense of gender and romantic love. Giddens also argues that change has come about because of the contraction in family size in the early twentieth century, and the availability of contraception, which resulted in a profound transition within personal life as 'sexuality became malleable, open to being shaped in diverse ways, and a potential 'property' of the individual' (Giddens, 1992: 27). For Foucault, discourse constitutes what it seeks to describe. Giddens is critical of the way that Foucault assumes this is a one-way process, as he regards the phenomenon as 'institutional reflexivity' (Giddens, 1992: 28), which is constantly in motion, and more open to agency than Foucault suggested. Giddens also writes that Foucault's discussion of the confessional is 'simply mistaken' (Giddens, 1992: 29), as therapy and psychoanalysis do not exist simply to regulate the confession of sex, rather they enable the exploration of the past and the individual's self-understanding.

The history of sexuality is both complex and contested. The unproblematic acceptance of a move from the repression to the liberalization of sexuality oversimplifies historical change and 'closes off from critical scrutiny such important features as the primacy of coitus as *the* outlet from sexual desire, the unconscious acceptance of heterosexuality as the epicentre of the erotic, the asexuality of children, and the gender-specific quality and direction of sexual desire' (Hawkes, 1996: 32). Recent scholarship (Dabhoiwala, 2012) dates a 'first' sexual revolution to mid-eighteenth century Britain, where Enlightenment thinking undermined religious authority by promoting the idea that people could expect to have a private life with sex belonging to that private realm. This would suggest that the shift from repression in the nineteenth century to liberalization in the mid-twentieth century is a false dichotomy.

Methodological Issues

The sweeping changes within all types of sexualities described above are of such seismic proportions that detecting them in an interview or focus group should be a straightforward task. However, the difficulties in differentiating between discourse and accurate descriptions of daily life proved to be an issue, as respondents were particularly nervous when discussing their sex lives, perhaps because of the perceived 'specialness of sex' (Hawkes, 1996: 5). Sex is taken to be the most intimate and private element of a relationship, and disclosing information about it to an interviewer may have made the respondents uncomfortable. To the younger couples, I asked the question 'is sex important to your relationship', as I felt that this allowed them to give as much information as they were comfortable with. While some respondents happily disclosed private details of their sex lives, others were visibly embarrassed and I moved the interview on. With the older respondents I asked the less personal question of whether they felt that attitudes towards sex in society had changed since during their lifetimes, as I was made to feel very aware of my youth and the need to be respectful in my questioning. It may have been that the older generation of respondents were less comfortable with public discussions of sexuality generally, or that they were reticent to discuss it with a younger woman, as other researchers have found (Hockey, Robinson and Meah, 2004).

The focus groups proved a more comfortable setting in which to discuss topics of sexuality, as they provided a more relaxed atmosphere in which participants were not directly asked personal questions, but instead participated within general group discussions. The older female focus group participants discussed changes in sexual norms in general, occasionally detailing the experiences of other relatives, but never explicitly referring to their own relationships.

The ethical and methodological issues associated with researching sex and sexuality undermine claims about the extent to which sex has been liberalized within contemporary western societies. For all of the challenges to traditional sexual mores the respondents here continued to understand sex as a private and unique aspect of their relationship.

The Role of Sex in Heterosexual Pair Relationships

In the interviews with the younger couples, sex is constructed as an essential part of the late modern heterosexual relationship, to the extent that not having sex is viewed as abnormal or deviant. A number of the respondents were quick to assert that the sexual aspects of their relationships were 'normal', which appeared to be measured in terms of vague statistics derived from the media on the frequency of intercourse:

'Yeah, of course sex is important, it would be weird if it wasn't, right?' (Niall, 5b)

'I can't imagine that if we didn't click in bed, you know if we weren't sexually compatible, that you would even start a relationship with someone, it's really a priority.' (Jane, 1a)

'Well, everyone knows that, from the papers, couples have sex twice a week, for the average couple, so you would compare yourself to that, I guess.'

Would it matter if you weren't having sex that often?
'Well, er, I suppose you would think something was wrong if you were doing it less.' (Paul, 9b)

'What's the average, like two or three times a week? Well, I'd say we were average, easily (laughs).' (Jeff, 7b)

The above extracts illustrate the importance of discourse in informing the ways couples think about and construct their sex lives, particularly for the two male respondents interviewed above who compare themselves to what they understand to be the national average. The production of statistics on sexual behaviour is particularly problematic (Gabb, 2010: 34), however it is apparent that they are often treated as incontrovertible 'facts' by which individuals and couples can and should measure themselves. The respondents here are reflexive to the extent that they compare their own experiences to what they perceive to be the norm, however this reflexivity has little to do with individual choice and freedoms.

The need to live up to a contemporary ideal does not represent freedom from repression, rather it alludes to different pressures as popular culture demands that we 'should become experts in sexual knowledge and fluent in sex talk' (Mac an Ghaill and Haywood, 2007: 150. Gail Hawkes has described how modern discourses on sexuality, while different in form to traditional conceptualizations, have a similar affect. Sex has become defined as the central dynamic of the late modern pair relationship and 'in this brave new age of sex, the greatest sin is sexual boredom' (Hawkes, 1996: 119).

The Male Sex Drive

The couples discuss sex in ways that utilize traditional and rigid constructions of highly differentiated male and female sexual needs, alluding to complex issues around power. The 'male sexual drive discourse' (Dallos and Dallos, 1997: 138), which relies on the assumption that men and women have biologically different sex drives, proved to be particularly important in shaping the ways couples talk about their relationships, relying on a stereotypical view of women as naturally passive and men as sexually aggressive. This discourse places pressure on women to 'allow' their partners to have sex with them, in return for emotional closeness. The male sexual drive discourse also places pressure upon the male partner to display a high sex drive, as maintaining his masculine identity relies on him being constantly ready for sex and there is no mention of men being 'too tired' for sex:

'Men have different drives, and can get turned on a lot quicker.' (Sam, 2b)

'I imagine that sex is more important to men, and er, intimacy is to women, you know men don't care if they have a hug afterwards, we just want to go to sleep (laughs).' (John, 4b).

'Men are always up for sex, aren't they?' (Teresa, 12a)

'Cause men are always up for it, you know.' (Alex, 12b)

Initially the findings indicate that sex is an area in which women appear to retain control, as they provide access to penetrative sex which my respondents' comments suggest men want. Within this discourse, as men are perceived to have higher sex drives female power stems from the idea that women control access to sex. Three of the younger men interviewed complained that their partners used sex for leverage within their relationships:

'It's like blow jobs, once you're living together, they tend to dry up, you get them as reward, not as a matter of course anymore.' (Ben, 6b)

'Yeah, but sexual equality and all that goes out the window when it comes to sex, that's where women control the relationship (laughs).' (Alex, 12b)

'Men have different drives, and can get turned on a lot quicker, so women can use sex as a power tool, definitely. It's like being teased, when you're in bed with someone, you know, and it's up to her whether you have sex or not.' (Sam, 2b)

The conceptualization of sex presented in these accounts suggests that it is something that men 'do' to women rather than an experience based on reciprocal pleasure. Although women are perceived to have power this is only ideological and it exists in tension with the ideology of the male sex drive. The latter, depending as it does on the notion that men need a certain amount of sex, bestows latent power on men as their partners strive accommodate their perceived needs. Additionally, any ideological power women have in controlling access to sex needs to be understood in the context of men's advantages on a structural level. Certain excerpts from the interviews with the younger women support this discourse, as sex is viewed as a chore rather than an area of the relationship that they enjoy control over:

'Well, because he works such long hours, then we have to find time for sex, you know, I have to say, turn the TV off, we'll go to bed.' (Jane, 1a)

'And, you know, we do have sex regularly, but sometimes I'm tired, and I don't feel like it. When we first started going out I was more experienced and I initiated things, but recently it's like a chore.' (Kate, 2a)

'In a relationship, sex is more about, err, just a quickie, you know for him to get off. The foreplay and exploring each other's bodies kind of fades (laughs).' (Chloe, 9a)

'It would be him that initiates it, you know, I can be tired, but you just feel awful saying no, you don't want to be one of those women that always has a headache, so it's easier to do it and just, you know, fake.' (Sara, 10a)

As well as being sexually available, some of the women interviewed described the pressure they felt to appear sexually desirable to their partners:

'He'll criticize me because of my weight, and tell me I need to go to the gym, and then the next minute he'll be like "do you fancy a shag?", and it's like "now let me think, you just basically called me a fat cow – do I feel sexy?".' (Kate, 2a)

Keeping one's partner sexually satisfied is understood to be part of a woman's duty, as these respondents not only provide their partners with sex but also anticipate their 'needs', which are prioritized above their own, revealing much about the power processes at work within heterosexual relationships. As Hawkes writes, 'good housekeeping has now been replaced by "good sex-making"' (Hawkes, 1996: 121), as a late modern feminine ideal. Female sexual pleasure appears to be important as Sara describes 'faking', suggesting that female climax is an important element of heterosexual sex. Women not only have to provide men with sex, but they must also reassure them of their sexual proficiency through the assimilation of pleasure (Rahman and Jackson, 2010: 189). The modern expectation that women should be sexually available and receptive has been accompanied by an obligation to exercise these desires through heterosexual sex (Hawkes, 1996: 108), which has retained its phallocentric framework in my respondents' definitions at least. In their extensive study of heterosexual relationships, Dunombe and Marsden (1996) found that women's emotional work extended to the bedroom, as their female respondents reported faking desire and agreeing to unwanted sex, much like the female participants in this study.

While the men and women interviewed frequently described the male sex drive as more powerful than female sexual desire, there were indications that for some of the couples this was reversed. What is particularly interesting is the tentative way in which this is alluded to:

'Er, I definitely want regular sex, but to be honest we do have a lot less. Sometimes I try to encourage Phil but he's not always up for it being tired from work.' (Emma, 11a)

'To be honest, I do worry sometimes, that he doesn't want sex as much anymore, maybe because I'm not as attractive as when we first met, because I was slimmer then, so that can make me feel a bit insecure sometimes.' (Carrie, 4a)

'I mean we do do it, but I feel like I'm the one that's pushing for it, which you don't expect when you're in a relationship, you expect to be harassed for it (laughs). It's hard to feel feminine and desirable if you're pressuring your boyfriend, sometimes I do wonder what's wrong with me that he doesn't want to do it more, I mean I have put on about a stone since we moved in together so I am scared that he finds me less attractive.' (Ali, 6a)

These female interviewees show dissatisfaction about the frequency of intercourse in their relationships, however they tend to see this as a result of external factors (for example their partner being tired from work) or blame themselves for not being sexually desirable enough, a finding that is supported by US-based research (Wyse, Smock and Manning, 2009) which found that heterosexual women tend to apologize for having higher sex drives than their male partners. Where popular discourses are not available for respondents to draw on, explaining their experiences becomes difficult and their accounts are laced with doubt. In particular there is the suggestion that women who fail to maintain a certain level of desirability are at fault for their partners' waning libidos. These respondents recognize their sexual desires as important and will initiate sexual contact with their partners, yet at the same time their actions are undermined by the 'should' of heterosexual partnerships. The male partners of the three women above made no reference to this issue and it was not addressed in any of the focus groups, yet it is obviously a source of misery and tension within these relationships.

Belief in the 'naturalness' of heterosexuality, with particular reference to 'natural' biological drives allow oppressive beliefs and practices to persist alongside more contemporary ideas about sexuality (Hockey, Robinson and Meah, 2002) and undermine emphases on female pleasure. There is little evidence here to support Giddens' claim that sex has been removed from the power of the phallus, at least within heterosexual relationships. The practicalities necessitated by living together appear to undermine the ideal of equality, in and out of the bedroom, while the 'marital' bed continues to be a scene of 'confusion and deception' (Jackson, 1996a: 72).

Although heterosexuality encompasses more than sex, the younger couples' traditional constructions of this area of their relationships allude to further inequalities. Contrasted with sexual experiences pre-relationship, the changes in women's experiences once in a long-term heterosexual relationship are striking.

Sexuality and Gender Identity

The younger women's sexual experiences within heterosexual relationships contrast in many cases with the way they behaved when single. Many women claimed that they were the more sexually experienced and promiscuous when they entered relationships with their current partners. In a reversal of traditional gender roles, these female respondents reported initiating sexual contact with their partners:

'Yeah, but it just kind of, it's like, we were kind of going out, but it was like just casual kind of dating, we were having sex, we weren't like 'let's have a relationship'. So, at that time I was in control, you can be selfish in that kind of situation, you know, sexually.' (Jane, 1a)

'Well, you know, you have to do the whole sleeping around thing at uni, 'cause that's how you learn what you like, and stuff, it's so much fun.' (Carrie, 4a)

'When we started seeing each other, I was more experienced, so you know, I got to show him what pleased me. Now there's much less foreplay.' (Kate, 2a)

'There aren't emotions involved when you're having casual sex, it's all about pleasure. In a relationship, it's more intimate, and you would be less concerned about your own pleasure than your partner's.' (Teresa, 12a)

The contrast between the reported behaviour of these women before they entered long term relationships with their experiences once in a relationship is striking. This situation appears to have parallels with the 1960s, when young single women were encouraged to explore their own sexuality by magazines such as *Cosmopolitan*, while married women living in the suburbs were ignored (Hawkes, 1996). While the younger women interviewed here are not mothers or full-time housewives, the effort involved in managing a relationship, a household and a career may come at the expense of sexuality and possibly other areas of personal development for the women interviewed:

> 'Sex just isn't the priority that it was when you were single, you know, you don't have time for all the foreplay, so you just get on with it. It's good still, but it's not that important to climax anymore, especially if it's going to take, like, forty minutes and I'm tired (laughs).' (Chloe, 9a)

While for young single women, sexual activity appears to have been liberalized, any period of promiscuity and experimentation is not expected to last as monogamy and a long term heterosexual relationship become the priority of these women. There are also limits to the sexual freedom exercised by the young women. Although Carrie is initially enthusiastic, she recounts a negative experience in her first year as a university student:

> 'I mean there are limits, I do think probably I went too far at times.'

> *In what way?*
> 'Well, for example when I was a fresher I had this really good group of male friends, next door to us in halls, we used to always hang out, I was always round their flat, but then I slept with two of them, not together obviously, but within about a month (laughs) and after that they stopped speaking to me. It was actually quite upsetting at the time, and it did make me feel, like, dirty or something and it did occur to me that I should be a bit more careful if I didn't want to be judged.' (Carrie, 4a)

Carrie's experiences here illustrate the continuing influence of the sexual double standard; 'young women continue to be vulnerable to negative identification as 'sluts' or 'slags' if they are too sexual' (Rahman and Jackson, 2010: 182). Heterosexual women have to carefully negotiate the line between appearing 'too' sexual and sexually passive or frigid.

The male focus group was revealing in this respect, in that the respondents note the difference between women they would seek out for casual sex and the behaviour they expect from the women they are in relationships with:

Is it acceptable for women to have casual sex?

B – It's preferable.

Group laughter

B – It depends on how many is a lot. Like this one girl, she'd had 140, and she was only twenty-three. I'm not sure if I'd want to make an honest woman of her, I mean she was fat and a minger.

Why did you have sex with her?

B – I wanted to get my numbers up (group laughter)

P – She just happened to be in the same toilet.

B – It's all true. It wasn't a meeting of souls.

(Male focus group, 20–35)

This dialogue indicates persistence of traditional attitudes towards male and female behaviour in and out of relationships. B had no qualms about coitus with a girl he found unattractive 'to get my numbers up'. While sleeping with a large number of women is a source of pride, similar behaviour in a woman is seen as problematic. At the same time as B's masculinity is bolstered enough for him to boast about the encounter to the group, his partner here is disparaged for her promiscuity. While men are expected to seek out women for recreational sex women, who succumb to this too easily are despised. Sexual permissiveness has increased, making it more acceptable for both heterosexual men and women to have sex outside of committed relationships. Yet this remains gendered as women are judged much more harshly than men for casual sex (England, 2010: 156).

Heterosexuality formed an unquestioned paradigm throughout the interviews and within the focus groups I specifically addressed the issue of sexuality. The younger women's dialogue went as follows:

Have you always known you were heterosexual?

J – I've never really thought about it.

C – Well you must have at some point.

J – No, I mean I've never had to, I've never felt otherwise, so I didn't have to think about it.

T – Yeah, I don't think it's something you have to sit down and think about, surely it's like an urge, or something.

(Female focus group, 20–35)

The participants describe sexuality as a biological urge, with heterosexuality as the default position. I asked the group whether any of them had had any sexual experiences with other women:

J – No way.

S – Well, you know, girls are always getting off with other girls, it's fashionable, or something.

J – Have you?

S – No.

C – I have (laughs).

J – Really?

S – What was it like?

C – It wasn't serious, me and a mate were drunk, this is in uni, and one of the guys we were with dared us to. I think it was more for his benefit than for ours.

S – Like Madonna and Britney, everyone knows they're straight, it was just for the pervy men watching.

(Female focus group, 20–35)

While C admits to kissing a female friend this is not seen as a lesbian act, rather something that was done for the pleasure of a heterosexual male friend. This encounter appears to have little to do with genuine sexual exploration or experimentation but is acted out because it is understood to be what men want (reflecting a popular trope in mainstream pornography). Ultimately this is can be interpreted as two women representing themselves as sexual objects for the gratification of a man, demonstrating how male sexual dominance continues to undermine female sexual pleasure (McKinnon, 2002). The idea that female empowerment is reflected in 'raunch culture' has been challenged by the writer Ariel Levy (2005), who maintains by making sex objects of themselves women are actually conforming to a commercialized, patriarchal construction of sexuality.

Within the male focus group there was constant banter about the other participants' sexuality, which perhaps indicates the performative nature of sexuality. Homosexuality appears to be a source of both fear and fascination, with participants keen to distance themselves from anything that could be interpreted as gay. When B attempts to make a serious point about male sexuality, he is teased by other members of the group:

B – Bisexuality, it's cool for women but definitely not for men. That's just not cool. However, I saw an interesting programme on prison, in the States, which changed my opinion of male sexuality. Basically there were all these prisoners and they all had sex with each other. There was this one guy who'd been in for years, and he was completely in love, he was like twenty stone, a proper crim, and he was saying it was the same as how he used to feel about women, and he now feels about this guy the same way.

P – You trying to tell us something? (group laughter)

P – I used to work in the gay village, and it was weird, men coming on to you.

A – The Turks are very gay, you know they only marry for procreation.

B – It was like that for the ancient Greeks, you know women were for babies, and boys were for fun.

P – Sounds like the sort of thing you'd have tattooed on your buttock, 'boys are for fun' (group laughter).

(Male focus group, 20–35)

Homosexuality is discussed in terms of the other by the participants, for example 'Turks', 'Greeks' and prisoners and never in any reference to their own sexuality, with bisexuality being 'cool' for women but not for men, possibly because of the ubiquity of 'lesbian' scenes in pornography marketed at heterosexual men. When one participant attempts to explain same-sex relationships in the context of an all-male environment he is teased by other group members, demonstrating how men are held accountable if they stray too far from the hegemonic form of masculinity (West and Zimmerman, 1989). While there is undoubtedly less stigma attached to homosexuality today, it remains marginalized by heteronormative cultures and is not the unproblematic choice for men that Giddens (1992) and Weeks (1995) suggest, as peer pressure and the existence of a heterosexual hegemonic masculine ideal (Connell, 1995) shape the discourses surrounding male sexuality.

The 'permissive discourse' (Hollway, 1996: 87), which influences the younger respondents' attitudes to sexuality, portrays sex as a matter of pleasure, and has a particular focus on the liberalization of female sexuality. The limitations of this discourse are apparent in my respondents' accounts with male and female sexual behaviour continuing to be interpreted differently. Sexuality is never really questioned by any of couples interviewed, as even the participant who has kissed another woman does not see this as detracting from her heterosexuality. Although heterosexuality has been largely uncoupled from monogamy and reproduction (Hawkes, 1996: 6) it retains a deep-seated connection with patriarchal sexual relations and continues to be privileged as the norm (Richardson and Monro, 2012: 17).

Monogamy

The recent public fascination and academic focus on consensual non-monogamy and polyamorous relationships (Barker and Langdridge, 2010) would suggest that dominant assumptions of the naturalness of monogamy may be being challenged. However, the accounts given in the interviews and focus groups here suggest that a pair relationship remains the only acceptable long-term sexual partnership. Infidelity is seen as universally negative:

'I would be heartbroken if Ian cheated on me, I mean I don't know if him, it would depend on whether we had kids you know.' (Jane, 1a)

'That's one thing, it's a dealbreaker for me, you just couldn't trust someone again if they did that.' (Niall, 5b)

'You just don't do that to someone you're supposed to be in love with, you know, how would you get past it in a relationship I don't know. People do I suppose but I don't know how.' (Sara, 10a)

'I can't say I've never been tempted, but you can't go there. There's no point being with someone if you want to be with someone else. With my ex I nearly cheated on her, but I realized I should just end it if I wasn't committed anymore.' (Alex, 12b)

The couple relationship is perceived to be the only legitimate sexual outlet for my respondents, with transgressions regarded as cause to potentially end the relationship. Rates of infidelity in heterosexual marriage are often stated as over 60 per cent (Robinson, 1997), yet anything other than lifelong monogamy is not openly tolerated. The discussions held in the older female focus group suggest women in longer term relationships are more pragmatic about the social reality of infidelity:

M – It's so important to be faithful, but then there are different circumstances.
A – Like what?
M – Well, my nephew, it turns out he's been having an affair for several years, but then he told my brother that his wife hasn't had sex with him for over four years. No, I mean that's not normal, so you can't really blame him.
A – Is there something wrong with her?
M – Well, she must need help.
(Female focus group, 50–65)

The male sexual drive discourse is again dominant here, with women displaying a shared understanding that men have a basic biological need for more sex than women, which may lead them to seek sexual partners outside of their relationship. Where women fail to provide their partners with enough sex they can expect them to stray. Based on interviews with 120 young men Eric Anderson (2012) claims that male sexual cheating is ubiquitous (78 per cent of his sample admit to sexual infidelity) and that the socially constructed monogamous ideal fails to satisfy the biological compulsion of male sexual urges. Cheating therefore becomes the rational response to the oppression of monogamy. Anderson suggests a sexually promiscuous, emotionally monogamous relationship as a more satisfactory solution. While monogamy may be a problematic ideal, Anderson promotes an understanding of sexuality that supports an essentialist understanding of the sex drives of men and women, which fails to recognize the extent to which sexuality and sexual behaviour is socially constructed. From a feminist perspective Victoria Robinson (1997) has argued that non-monogamy in heterosexual relationships may be a way for women to exercise their agency and desire in defiance of dominant institutionalized heterosexuality. Evidence would suggest that heterosexual women also struggle with sexual fidelity; a third of the members of AshleyMadison.com, a notorious dating site designed to facilitate extramarital affairs, are women, with female membership increasing at a faster rate than male (Caplan, 2009). Either way, while the dominant ideal of monogamy within heterosexual partnerships fails to account for the reality of sexual infidelity it will continue to be a source of relationship conflict and breakdown.

Positive Pleasures

There are a number of discourses surrounding sexuality within heterosexual relationships and a common theme was sex as an expression of love. Both male and female respondents describe sex with their partners as a powerful experience:

'When you love someone, sex can be just so, er, well it can just blow your mind how much you love that person.' (Alex, 12a)

'If you make the effort, you know if it's not just a quickie because its Saturday morning and he's feeling horny, then sex can just be so good, make you feel so connected.' (Carrie, 4a)

'God, no, if I don't feel like sex then we don't have it, he knows he has to make an effort, I am so not the sort of person who lies back and thinks of England (laughs). God, why do women do that?' (Christie, 5a)

'It's like a different type of sex when you're single, you don't care about the other person, when you love them, then it's much more special, even if you don't feel the same kind of, um, lust.' (Jane, 1a)

Sex does also function as an expression of love and intimacy within long term relationships and is described as an intimate, reciprocal experience, which suggests that it is possible for men and women to meet as equals (Hollway, 1996). While remaining critical of dominant frameworks of heterosexuality we can allow for 'the element of pleasure in heterosexual practices' (Segal, cited in Smart, 1996: 175).

Morality, Promiscuity and the Sexual Revolution

The sexual revolution of the 1960s and 70s is generally viewed as the watershed in the liberalization of heterosexuality, both within academic and popular discourse; as Philip Larkin lyricized, 'Sexual intercourse began in nineteen sixty-three' (*Annus Mirabilis*, 1967). These decades will have provided the context within which the older respondents would have had their first sexual experiences. However, for many of these respondents, the sexual revolution was something that they were aware of, yet which they felt did not affect them directly:

'It's hard to explain, but we knew things were going on, and while you might have got away with things in London, it wasn't acceptable here, so it didn't really affect me.' (Barbara, 25a)

'Well, I had a mini skirt, I had the figure for it then, but my dad was livid, and I never did anything, we wanted to look fashionable, but the most experience I had before my twenties was kissing a poster of Paul McCartney (laughs).' (Ann, 23a)

'There were girls, you know who lived with their boyfriends before they got married, but I would never have done it, my mother would have killed me. Because I was a stewardess, we had night stops in hotels, and all sorts of things went on, you wouldn't believe it. But at home, you had to act respectably.' (Marie, 22a)

The older women interviewed acknowledge the importance of respectability at the time they were growing up, and are keen to stress their own chasteness. This did not appear to apply to young men at the time:

'Well, in the seventies, if you'd been living with a girl, then her name would have been mud. There's no way you'd live together or have children without being married, you'd have been, well no one would have talked to you.' (Trevor, 21b)

'I was a pilot, you know, I lived with girls, it was the 1960s. But I don't think their parents knew. And you wouldn't have married those types of girls, anyway, you didn't have to.' (Anton, 22b)

Again, respectability is only applied to women, as masculinity is untainted, or even bolstered by promiscuity. The women who did cohabit with their partners are described as 'those types of girls', whose 'name would have been mud', by Anton and Trevor respectively. This view has parallels with the description of a promiscuous girl in the younger male focus group as not someone 'I'd want to make an honest woman of' (B). While younger women enjoy relatively more sexual freedom than the older women interviewed, there remain limits which do not appear to apply to men.

The older respondents were particularly garrulous when discussing the changes in sexual practices, with most regarding the perceived changes as negative:

'Girls today seem to do things we would never have dreamt of. I had a couple of boyfriends before I met my husband, but I would never have lived with them, and I would never have, I would never have had one night stands, or whatever you call them.' (Barbara, 25a)

'I think girls are much more promiscuous now, you know, it can go a bit far. But then I don't know if that's changed, I mean that type of girl has always been around.' (Fiona, 21a)

Barbara and Fiona are both critical of young women's sexuality, but do not apply this morality to young men. Again, there is the disparagement of promiscuous women as 'that type of girl', however, in this instance it comes from a female respondent. Homosexuality is also discussed by an older female respondent:

'Things have changed so much since I was growing up, especially with, well gay men and women. I mean I had heard of them, but it was seriously disapproved of, you know, something you would hide, and now they're everywhere. It's better really, because they're born that way, you know it's not something they can help, but I wouldn't want one of my sons to be gay, not with diseases.' (Liz, 24a)

Liz is accepting of homosexuality, as she regards it as a biological disorder which 'they' cannot help. The stereotypical links between homosexuality and (sexually transmitted) disease are a reason for Liz to hope that her son is not gay without appearing homophobic. While Liz is not overtly critical of homosexuality, she describes gay men and women as having a genetic disorder, for which they should be pitied.

One of the older respondents viewed increased freedoms more favourably:

'Young women today can get away with a lot more today than we could, I think it's better that they can live with partners before getting married, you've got more choice today.' (Ann, 23a)

Her use of word 'we' suggests that Ann considers her experience part of a wider generational identity. She is the only respondent with an uncritical view of women's freedom to cohabit, possibly because she had daughters in their twenties at the time of the interview.

The sexual revolution is dated from the 1960s; however the interviewees here describe it as a discourse that did not affect their everyday lives, a finding which supports more sceptical views of the social changes of the time (Hawkes, 1996). Even the more vocal proponents of the sexual revolution, such as the writer Erica Jong, now concede that it was 'mainly a media myth' (Jong, 2000). While women were expected to act respectably, heterosexual male promiscuity is regarded as unproblematic. All of the respondents feel that female sexuality has been liberalized within recent years, although only one respondent views this as a positive development, with the rest seeing it as a cause for concern.

The older women are also aware of the pressures of 'good sex-making', although they avoid referring to their own sex lives instead preferring to reflect on the actions of others, in particular promiscuous women, gay men and the 'younger generation'. Both generations of respondents view the other in terms of popular stereotypes:

P – Comparable to the 70s they were shagging in the streets weren't they?
J – Yeah, it was one big orgy.
(Male focus group, 20–35)

'But, like the sixties generation, it was all 'free love' wasn't it? I mean, not my parents, they were bloody traditional, but most people.' (Jane, 1a)

The 'sixties generation' is viewed as liberal in terms of sexuality, and the 1970s is described as 'one big orgy', however, Jane inadvertently describes the differences between ideology and experience, as her example of the practice of this generation are her 'bloody traditional' parents, who do not conform to the popular stereotype. Similarly, older respondents interpret young peoples' relationships as more egalitarian than my findings suggest. The fixed, unequal institution of marriage is the basis of my older respondents' relationships, and the elevation of the 'respectable' women remains apparent in discussions about sexuality.

Summary

Analysis of the participants' accounts indicate that sexual experiences have changed between the generations, as young men and women are now expected to have a number of sexual partners before committing to a long term heterosexual relationship. The older respondents have a largely negative view of this, as although behaviour may have been similar in their youth it was not openly practiced as the ideal of the 'respectable woman' had to be maintained. While the older respondents belong to the 'sixties generation', for the women interviewed this was a discourse they were aware of, but which they felt unable to incorporate into their everyday lives because of social pressures.

Once in heterosexual relationships, the younger respondents are pressured by constant surveys published in the media, detailing, for example, the amount of times per week that the average couple has sex. While certain elements of heterosexuality appear to remain unchanged, there have undoubtedly been changes in perceptions of the role of sex in relationships. Reproduction is not alluded to by any of the respondents within the context of sex and while the majority of younger couples express the wish to have children at some point, the connection between sex and reproduction, if not completely severed, appears to be suspended until couples choose to start a family. Discourses on sex and sexualities remain heteronormative and phallocentric, with coitus regarded as essential to a couple relationship. Sex is referred to exclusively in this context, with no reference to auto-eroticism or alternative sexual practices. As with other areas of the relationship the pressure is on the female partner to ensure that her man is satisfied, as it is assumed that men automatically want more sex than their partners. Where the reverse is true it is a source of embarrassment and shame. Intimacy and equality within my respondent's relationships are undermined by their traditional understandings of masculinity and femininity, as shifts in the outward forms of heterosexuality have done little to change heterosexual practice (Hawkes, 1996). Couples view their sex lives as intensely private, and beyond the realm of the social, in spite of evidence to the contrary, meaning that attention is focussed upon individual relationships, rather than the structures which constrain and limit them (Jackson, 1993: 202).

Heterosexuality is not a fixed entity and there is evidence of the 'mutual recognition' described by Hollway (1996: 105) which allows men and women to enjoy sex as equals, however, the findings suggest that combined with these changes are continuities related to normative masculine and feminine roles. Taken for granted essentialist ideas that the male sex drive is dominant and that heterosexual sex is 'the mature and normal form of sex' (Rahman and Jackson, 2010: 29) exert a strong influence over my respondents' accounts. Pre-relationship, promiscuity is a source of pride for both generations of male respondents, however, while the younger generation of women have increased sexual freedom, this has limits in terms of the amount of men they are able to have sex with before becoming a 'slag'. This sexual freedom also apparently maintains heteronormative ideals, as my respondents have all ultimately ended up in heterosexual relationships. However, the men here are not essentially oppressive as they show no desire to subjugate their partners, particularly as when many of the younger respondents' relationships began the female partner was the more sexually experienced. As Smart (1996) has argued, heterosex may not be the primary element of female oppression, but the practices encompassed within heterosexual relationships, which range far beyond the sexual (Jackson, 1996b), may be key to the lasting inequalities evident in both generations of relationships studied. The authors of detraditionalized sexualities do not always consider the investments that men and women have with traditional notions of masculinity and femininity, which undermine late modern notions of reflexivity (McNay, 1999). The next chapter shifts the focus from sexuality to the role and construction of love and intimacy within couple relationships.

Chapter 6
What's love got to do with it? Doing Intimacy

The importance with which communication, or mutual disclosure, is afforded within late modern relationships is explored in this chapter. I develop a detailed understanding of what is represented by the term intimacy within both sociological understanding and the popular discourses that influence the couples interviewed. Intimacy and communication are addressed within the same chapter as a result of their bracketing within the late modern ideal of disclosing intimacy; as Giddens maintains 'intimacy presumes self-disclosure' (Giddens, 1992: 139). Love as a central component of intimacy is also reflected upon as 'Conceptually, 'love' and 'intimacy' are close relatives' (Jamieson, 2011: 3.3). The methodological challenges of assessing intimacy and communication within the participants' relationships are discussed, followed by a breakdown of the interview and focus group data which focuses on gender and generational differences in expressions of intimacy.

Defining Intimacy

Lynn Jamieson (1998, 2011) engages in a discussion of what is meant by 'intimacy' and its relevance to contemporary understandings of relationships. Intimacy usually refers to a specific sort of 'knowing, loving and 'being close' to another person' (Jamieson, 1998: 1), with a modern emphasis on talking, listening and sharing thoughts and feelings, which Jamieson terms 'disclosing intimacy' (ibid). Jamieson critically examines the notion that this type of intimacy, which relies on mutual disclosure and intense communication, is heavily promoted within therapeutic literature and is characterized by Giddens' pure relationship, lies at the centre of late modern personal life. She questions the extent to which late modernity has transformed intimate relationships as disclosing intimacy is dependent upon individuals engaging as equals and transcending traditional structural inequalities within their relationships.

For proponents of late modern forms of intimacy, such as Giddens, communication in the form of 'mutual disclosure' is crucial. This intense dialogue provides the only anchor for contemporary relationships with traditional ties no longer available to fall back on, meaning that couples have to negotiate every element of their relationship; 'Issues are discussed, rather than driven underground' (Giddens, 1998: 125). Giddens defines intimacy as 'above all a matter of emotional communication in a context of interpersonal equality' (Giddens, 1992: 130).

The emphasis placed upon communication and self-disclosure as the central components of intimacy has led Duncombe and Marsden (1993) to suggest that a premium has been placed upon individuals' ability to 'do' intimacy. Late modern forms of intimacy involve emotional action, rather than mere 'being' (Duncombe and Marsden, 1993: 222). Their research of sixty couples provides an account of the gender differences and divisions in the emotional labour involved in love and intimacy. While value has been placed upon the ability to communicate, individuals' capacities to express emotion are socially regulated, meaning that men and women have differing abilities in making the emotional effort necessary. Duncombe and Marsden note that this may become a cause of conflict for couples as heterosexual women often feel that their partners lack 'emotional participation' in their relationships. The majority of their female respondents described experiencing an asymmetry of emotional response within their relationships (Duncombe and Marsden, 1993: 225). Respondents' reactions to this asymmetry took several forms. Some women insisted that they really were satisfied, perhaps in an attempt to conform to the popular ideal, however most were ready to blame themselves for expecting too much from their partners, a finding that Duncombe and Marsden believe is supported by the bestselling status of self-help books such as Robin Norwood's *Women Who Love Too Much* (1988). Male respondents reacted to women's demands with incomprehension or avoidance and displayed a tendency to intellectualize arguments rather than engage with their partners on the emotional level that they required.

From their findings Duncombe and Marsden maintain that there are two types of gender differences in emotion work. The first is the susceptibility to and valuation of romantic discourse and intimacy, with women tending to attach more importance to this than men. The second is the ability and willingness to disclose emotionally and 'do' intimacy. While women are often seen within popular discourse to be emotional, masculine ideals prioritize rational thought, meaning that men have not learnt to do intimacy in the same way that women have and that male friendships provide no rehearsal for this type of emotional disclosure (Mansfield and Collard, 1988).

Theorists have largely concurred with the image of men as 'emotionally stunted'. Giddens describes men as the 'laggards' of the transformation of intimacy, and women as 'the emotional revolutionaries of modernity' (Giddens, 1992: 130). He argues that men have problems with intimacy because of their schismatic view of women and the lapsed emotional narrative of the self that men may suffer from. However, I would challenge the assumption that women are more able to be intimate than men solely on the basis of their gender, as it may lead one to devalue male emotional participation within their intimate relationships and place further pressure upon women to do all of the emotional labour within their relationships. I would agree with Jackson (1993) that women and men do probably experience love differently, however it does not follow that one gender experiences love at a deeper level that the other. Most discourses of gender, sexuality and love represent women as more deeply emotive beings, as well as being more nurturant and expressive (Jackson, 1993: 214). Furthermore, part of the culture of romance is women's shared knowledge of men's emotional illiteracy (Jackson, 1993: 216).

Francesca Cancian (1987) writes that the argument that women are more loving than men serves to reinforce gender stereotypes rather than undermine them, as gender differences in love should diminish with other forms of gender inequality. Cancian is also sceptical of studies that have supported the idea that women are more loving, as she argues that they are biased by the feminized definition of love. It may be true that women have closer friendships, stronger kinship ties and are more skilled at expressing their feelings, however, men have their own style of love that emphasizes practical assistance, shared activities and sexual gratification, although this is not always defined as love because men's emotional behaviour is measured with a feminine ruler (Cancian, 1987: 74–5). Defining love as feminine serves to devalue male expressions of love, yet ultimately it is most damaging to women as it overlooks the work involved in maintaining relationships and continues to locate love in the private sphere while legitimating more exploitative relations amongst men in the outside world.

Love is a particularly complex dimension of intimacy which is nevertheless a priority for couples when establishing a relationship. The value placed on love may be particularly high within individualized western cultures that have weaker kinship ties (Simmons, Kolke and Shimizu, 1986). As Lewis (2001: 5) notes, it would be considered very strange if a Western couple did not place being in love at the top of their list of reasons for marrying as love appears to have moved from an ideal to an expectation Evans, 2003). However, there has been little research of the experiences and meanings of love, possibly because it is largely understood as a presocial emotion which is too individual and personal to be subjected to sociological analysis (Jackson, 1993: 202). Beall and Sternberg (1995: 417) decry sterile academic definitions of love that 'always seem incomplete and dry versions of a sometimes explosive experience, which might cause the reader to wonder if the author of the definition has ever been in love.'

Although romantic convention portrays love as indefinable, a feeling that can be known only intuitively and cannot be accurately described (Jackson, 1993: 207), the love that individuals want, expect and feel they need throughout their lives is a complex social construction which varies historically and socially

(Jamieson, 1998: 9). Although the experience of being in love may feel personal it is always constructed through language, narrative and stories (Wetherell, 1995). Jamieson illustrates this by pointing out that over the past century love has become much more demonstrative, although this does not mean that it is necessarily experienced on a deeper level. This is perhaps another example of the cult of disclosing intimacy; being in love is not enough, as one has to actively express that love. Jackson notes the difference in the love felt for a family member, and the experience of 'falling in love' with a sexual partner (Jackson, 1993: 207). While the initial rush of passion and lust individuals feel when 'falling in love' helps in selecting a partner, in a successful relationship this is expected to develop into lasting affection and companionship (ibid). Sex is often viewed as an expression of love, as couples who enjoy both love and sex in their relationships are portrayed as on a higher plane of happiness (Jamieson, 1998: 108). Love is also linked with care, although relying on a loved one for care is at odds with the ideal of the free-floating pure relationship (Jamieson, 1998: 10). While I would argue for an understanding of love as socially constructed, following Jackson (1993) I believe that individuals do not passively accept this, rather we create for ourselves a sense of what love is by engaging in the discourses surrounding it. Love is a constant focus of not only great works of art, but also television programmes, novels, magazines and popular music, which provide us with the scripts to construct our own experiences in narrative form although these are scripts that we can modify and subvert (Jamieson, 2011: 4.5). Ideals of love are constantly reproduced, forming part of our larger cultural imagination (Evans, 2003) and are therefore an important subject for sociological research.

Methodological Issues

In 1976, Arlie Hochschild first made the case for a sociology of emotions, writing that feelings had been neglected because they are often seen as private and individual and therefore presocial in some way. She acknowledged the difficulties in evaluating respondents' emotions, as 'feeling might seem impossible to capture in the loose net of sociological instruments' (Hochschild, 1976: 283). She suggested that as people perform 'emotion work' (Hochschild, 1976: 290) on their feelings by continually socializing their feelings according to the specific social context that they are in, sociologists should examine actors' own definitions of their emotions in order to find out what emotional vocabularies are used, what inner experiences they refer to and which social situations they apply to. Following Hochschild, the participants were questioned about the importance of meaningful communication to their relationships and their responses were analysed for evidence of the influence of the social on private issues. This approach was particularly useful in considering the role of love in relationships, as I asked my respondents whether love was important and what it meant to them. Rather than attempting to define love objectively the research focuses on its subjective meaning for the couples interviewed. The emotions displayed by respondents within the interviews are also considered, and contrasted with the behaviour of the participants in the focus groups.

The difficulties I encountered in researching love and intimacy should not detract from the importance of pursuing these areas within sociological investigation; their neglect is something that this research seeks to help remedy.

Gender Differences in Communication

The intense communication demanded by modern types of intimacy may have resulted in an increase in the amount of 'emotional labour' (Hochschild, 1989) undertaken, particularly by women, who often take on the responsibility of managing their relationship. This may be because women are more skilled in emotion work and value it more highly (Duncombe and Marsden, 1993), or possibly as a result of the definition of love as feminine (Cancian, 1987), which upholds love as a female responsibility. The findings from the younger generation suggest that women do place a higher value on communication, although many insist that they initiate attempts to talk about their feelings but are often rebuffed by their partners who feel that they are being nagged or pressured, as Jane explains:

'I would like to discuss things more, but Ian hates talking about things, so I don't do it as often as we should.' (Jane, 1a)

This suggests an outside pressure to communicate as part of the late modern relationship ideal. Jane is caught between wanting to communicate because she feels she 'should', and not wanting to annoy her partner, illustrating a gulf between ideology and practice. Rather than passively withdrawing from their relationships as reported in other research (Langford, 1999: 87), many of the younger women pressure their partners into verbalizing their feelings and refuse to accept male reticence to talk:

'I'm always trying to discuss things more, but Sam finds communication difficult.' (Kate, 2b)

'Oh my God, communication is so important to me, I like to discuss everything, I think it's really important, but Alex just can't do it. I really try to make him talk about his feelings, but he finds it so hard.' (Teresa, 12a)

'You know it's really important to me to communicate, and talk about things, but men just aren't good at it. I try, but it's so much effort, it's like getting blood out of a stone, you know (laughs).' (Chloe, 9a)

Chloe's description reflects the popular stereotype that it is the female partner who drives the heterosexual relationship, as men are naturally less skilled at emotional communication. She describes her efforts to encourage her partner to talk as 'like getting blood out of a stone', reflecting a traditional view of men's inability to show their feelings. Similarly, Kate places the fault for lack of emotional communication at the feet of the man in the relationship who finds communication 'difficult'. Teresa expresses frustration at her partner's inability to express his feelings, particularly as communication is important to her. One interviewee describes how she forces her partner to open up to her:

'I communicate enough for both of us (laughs). No, I always tell Niall what I'm thinking, and I force him to talk about stuff, although he'd probably rather not.' (Christie, 5a)

Christie was open and direct throughout the interview, which appears to reflect her attitude to her relationship. She portrays herself as the dominant partner who controls the relationship and forces a reluctant Niall to talk to her about his feelings.

Three of the younger female respondents complained about the pressures they felt to communicate, in order to live up to the late modern ideal of a 'good' relationship. Unlike the other women interviewed, who described communication as a personal need, these respondents felt an external pressure which left them with a dissatisfaction they may not have experienced otherwise:

'It's one of those things that you feel you should do more, you know magazines are always going on about how important it is, but it just takes so much effort, you know, who's got time to analyse every aspect of their relationship.' (Sara, 10a)

'We don't talk about things as much as we should, because we just end up arguing.' (Michelle, 8a)

'We don't analyse things, or have relationship 'talks', but sometimes I do feel we should try to communicate more.' (Anna, 3a)

Anna talks of feeling that she 'should' have deeper talks with her partner. Her feelings seem to stem from wanting to conform to a popular ideal, rather than from any dissatisfaction she has with her relationship. Earlier in the interview she complained about the lack of practical help she received from her partner, which would seem to be more important to her than increased levels of communication. Michelle also believes that she 'should' talk to her partner more, although she is nervous of the conflict it can cause. Sara complained about the pressures she felt to constantly communicate with her partner and admitted that she didn't always feel like analysing her relationship. This was in contrast to the other respondents who refer to their partners' reticence for the lack of communication within their relationships, suggesting that as women they feel they should want to talk about their feelings. Being emotional is considered to be part of being feminine and within this context admitting that she is not particularly interested in emotional communication is brave, although Sara defends herself as not having the time rather than not wanting to talk.

Another respondent maintained that she did not need to discuss every aspect of life with her partner, as long as the 'important stuff' was covered:

'We talk about important stuff, you know, but we don't tell each other every little thing.' (Carrie, 4a)

One of the few female respondents who felt that her partner was skilled at communication expressed a certain amount of disillusion, as she felt that talking was meaningless without practical change. In this sense communication alone cannot sustain a relationship:

'Ben's not too bad, actually, we communicate quite well, but I'm not convinced that it actually achieves anything, you know. It's like we talk about housework, and he knows my feelings, but it doesn't actually change his behaviour.' (Ali, 6a)

Only two of the younger couples interviewed stressed the importance of communication to their relationships:

'Communication is so important to our relationship, we talk about everything, you know, all our feelings. We often spend the whole night talking, so we don't get any sleep (laughs).' (Dawn, 7a)

'Oh, it's hugely important. I don't see how you can have a relationship without communication, well not a good relationship, anyway.' (Jeff, 7b)

Jeff and Dawn both maintain the importance of communication to their relationship, to the extent that they feel superior to other couples. Their answers are similar, which may indicate that one partner 'primed' the other about the question. They appear very eager to conform to the relationship ideal of constant communication, and it is not clear whether this, or a genuine desire to share their feelings, is their main motivation. Similarly, Emma and Phil express pride at their lack of secrets:

'Yes, we talk about everything, we don't have any secrets.' (Emma, 11a)

'Yes, you know we're adults, you can't have a relationship without communication.' (Phil, 11b)

Other male respondents display a reluctance to communicate, although many of them grudgingly acknowledge the importance of this aspect of their relationship:

'I don't see the point in talking about everything, but we do discuss the important stuff.' (Ian, 1b)

'We talk if we have to.' (Mark, 8b)

'Well, yeah, I think it's important, but women seem to feel the need to communicate all the time, whereas men don't. Is it a reassurance thing, I don't know?' (John, 4b)

Ian and John both admit that communication is important, suggesting that they are also influenced by relationship ideals, however John complains about women's (in general, not just his partner's) need to 'communicate all the time', perhaps because of their insecurity. He states broadly that 'men don't', indicating that this is part of a general masculine identity that he identifies with. Ben reiterates the point that women 'always' want to talk:

'Yeah, I can talk about things, sure, but Ali wants to talk after sex, or whatever, when you just don't feel like it.' (Ben, 6b)

Paul describes communication as important but goes on to qualify this as important to his partner rather than himself:

'Communication, yeah, it's important, Chloe likes to talk about things.' (Paul, 9b)

One respondent expresses relief that he does not have to overanalyse his relationship, although he concedes the importance of communicating with his partner:

'Of course we communicate, we tell each other things, but, you know we don't dissect every aspect of the relationship, thank God.' (Steven, 10b)

Niall insinuates that he is insincere in his communication with his partner, as he 'just tells her what she wants to hear', rather than engaging in the deep and meaningful level of mutual disclosure demanded by Christie:

'Women always want to talk about "the relationship", it just gets so boring. Don't tell Christie that, she makes me talk, so I just tell her what she wants to hear (laughs). No, I can see the point in communicating, but you don't need to talk about every bloody thing, you know.' (Niall, 5b)

Two of the younger male respondents lament their inability to talk about their relationships:

'Oh no, Teresa likes to talk about her feelings all the time, and she's always trying to get me to talk about how I feel, and I feel bad, but I'm just not as emotional as her. I keep telling her, football is my emotional release, but she just doesn't get it. She can't accept that I don't want to cry every five minutes, but men just aren't as emotional.' (Alex, 12b)

Alex perceives a gender difference in the way that he and Teresa handle their emotions. While she is eager to discuss things with him, he sees football as his emotional release. He argues that he is not as emotional as his partner; however, using football as an outlet for his emotions suggests that he is emotional, but he has found a release that is socially acceptable and does not compromise his masculine identity.

'Kate tried to talk about the relationship, but I just find it so difficult, I get frustrated that I can't express myself that well.' (Sam, 2b)

Sam describes not having the necessary skills to discuss his feelings, which does not mean that he is not emotional, but that as a man he has never learnt how to communicate.

Generally, communication is uncritically accepted as an important part of their relationships by the majority of the respondents, although there are gender differences in descriptions of the amount of communication needed. In this sense, 'communication' can be defined as a 'hurrah word' (Cohen, 1985, cited in Hockey, Robinson and Meah, 2002: 6.4) that elicits a universally positive response. Only one male respondent argues against the need to communicate, suggesting it is only something he and his partner would do if their relationship were unsatisfactory:

'I don't think we really need to talk about things, really, we're happy as we are.' (Carl, 3b)

The gender differences in the valuation of and ability to communicate is more pointed in the focus groups. The younger women despaired at their partners' lack of communication skills, displaying a shared understanding of male emotional illiteracy (Jackson, 1993: 216):

Is communication more important to women?
J – Do you need to ask?
S – Definitely.
C – It's always an effort to get men to talk, they just don't seem comfortable with it, like it's gay or something.
A – Yeah, but girls, I went out with this one guy who always wanted to talk about his feelings, it was awful.
J – You're kidding, I would love for Ian to be able to talk about things more.
A – No, trust me, this guy would like cry after sex and stuff. (group laughter)
C – God, that's awful.
A – Tell me about it.
(Female focus group, 20–35)

While the participants initially insist that they would like their partners to communicate more, they are horrified by A's story of an emotional ex-boyfriend, particularly because of his tendency to cry. Masculinity is as important to women as it is to men, and displays of emotion such as this, which compromise a man's masculine identity, are considered unacceptable by the female participants. Although the women insist that they would like their partners to be more emotional this is not unqualified and has to be carefully balanced with their partner's heterosexual masculinity.

The male focus group also referred to traditional gender stereotypes:

Is communication more important to women?
J – Fuck yes.
(Group laughter)
B – It's like gravity, it's just a fact.
A – Women always want to talk, especially when the football's on.
B – Or after sex, when you just want to go to sleep.
Why do you think this is?
J – I think they're just more emotional.
A – Definitely.
(Male focus group, 20–35)

It is taken for granted by the men that women are more emotional than they are, although within the context of the focus group it would have been difficult for any of the participants to admit that communication is important to them.

While Western masculinity is not constituted as wholly unemotional, men are not encouraged to develop competence in locating themselves within emotional discourses (Jackson, 1993: 214). Hollway (1996) argues that discourses of masculinity and femininity socialize men and women into very different roles, which protect male power and repress the needs that men share in common with women. Unable to accept their own emotional responses, men project their weakness and dependency onto their female partner. Men are both excluded and exclude themselves from the culture of romance in order to maintain a sense of heterosexual masculinity, which depends on sexual conquest rather than romance.

The Importance of Communication for the Older Respondents

The older respondents appear to attach less value to communication, and appear to feel less pressure to live up to disclosing intimacy, although the five couples sampled all have differing responses:

> 'Well, of course communication is important, when you've been together this long you can talk about everything, but then Trevor doesn't always like to talk about his feelings. But my mum and dad, well they never seemed to talk at all, you know it wasn't done in those days.' (Fiona, 21a)

Fiona indicates that the longevity of her relationship with her husband means that she feels able to be open with him, although, possibly because he is a man he 'doesn't always like to talk about his feelings'. Comparing her relationship favourably with that of her parents hints that Fiona may feel a generational identity which separates her from older generations. Communication would appear to have increased in importance for each generation according to Fiona. Trevor interprets communication as referring to any kind of conversation, rather than as a deeper disclosure about his emotions. This may indicate that he is less influenced by the emphasis placed upon emotional communication by late modern discourses on relationships:

> 'Yes we communicate, that's a funny question, how would we get by if we didn't talk?' (Trevor, 21b)

Within Marie and Anton's relationship, Anton appears to take on the emotional labour of constantly reassuring his anxious wife:

'Because I'm a bit of a worrier, I have to talk to Anton about things, because otherwise I can get upset, and he's brilliant, he's so strong, he always sorts things out and makes me feel better.' (Marie, 22a)

The interviews so far have built up a picture of emotion work as a female responsibility, whereas here we can see a husband attending to his wife's emotional needs. This does not, however, extend to Anton being able to share his own feelings:

'I talk to Marie if she needs me, but I don't need to talk, I'd rather spend the time doing something.' (Anton, 22b)

Although Anton manages his wife's emotion, he seems to view it as a feminine weakness that he does not allow in himself. Anne describes not needing to discuss feelings because she has been married for so long that her and her partner have developed an unspoken understanding. This is in contrast to the ideal of disclosing intimacy; however it would appear that both partners are happy in their relationship. This is reiterated by Patrick:

'Yes, of course, we discuss things, like how the girls are doing, how the business is doing. I don't suppose we talk about our feelings that much, because when you've been together so long you know what the other is thinking, really.' (Anne, 23a)

'I can talk about anything with Anne, I just don't have to.' (Patrick, 23b)

Taking one's partner for granted in this way is the antithesis of Giddens' pure relationship, although it has not had a negative impact upon this marriage. Jamieson (1998) has argued that love and affection can be demonstrated in multiple ways, with disclosing intimacy as only one possibility, I would suggest that Anne and Patrick's relationship is evidence of this.

In contrast to Anne, Liz displays discontent at the lack of communication in her relationship with her husband:

'No, I do try to talk more, but Joe just can't seem to do it. He never really says anything nice, I mean I know he loves me, but he never tells me. I suppose that's what you expect after twenty-five years, you can't expect someone to change.' (Liz, 24b)

That Liz's husband has difficulty in discussing his feelings may be the reason he avoided being interviewed. Unlike other couples who have developed an unspoken intimacy, Liz wants her husband to verbalize his feelings for her.

Barbara has previously hinted that she is insecure in her relationship, as she is worried about her husband leaving her for a younger woman, and retaining an element of 'mystery' appears to be part of her efforts to remain alluring.

> 'Um, I suppose so, although you can't tell your partner everything, you've got to retain some mystery.' (Barbara, 25a)

To Barbara, staying married to her successful husband is more important than disclosing her emotions. This is not a pressure expressed by any of the other respondents, perhaps because the younger generation of women have professional identities in their own right and do not need the support of a wealthy husband in this sense. Richard, Barbara's husband is characteristically dismissive:

> 'Yes, we communicate when we have to.' (Richard, 25b)

While the younger respondents shared similar reactions, the smaller mature sample has illustrated how unique relationships are in practice. As Jamieson (1998) has noted, despite the late modern emphasis upon this type of intimacy, 'disclosing intimacy' is not 'becoming the crux of personal life as it is lived' (Jamieson, 1998: 158). 'Disclosing intimacy' is unimportant to the older couples interviewed, possibly because the length of their relationships has fostered unspoken understandings. This is in contrast to the younger couples, for whom the discourse of disclosing intimacy is an ideal to which they aspire, although their inability to always do so may result in dissatisfaction with their relationships. The romance narratives employed by the older respondents are distinct from those that influence the younger couples. This may be linked to the two cohorts' distinct generational identities and cultural positionings, or may have more to do with their different positions within the life course. The older couples have all been together for around thirty years, which may lead to a different kind of intimacy to that enjoyed by the younger couples, who have been together for an average of five years.

Love

The role and importance of love in my respondents' relationships proved a complex issue. As Lewis (2001) argues, love is at the top of the list of reasons for getting married or cohabiting. All of my respondents, within both generations, answered in the affirmative when I asked whether love was important to their relationship, as the following quotes from the younger respondents illustrate:

'Of course, that's why you're together.' (Jane, 1a)

'It goes without saying.' (Ian, 1b)

'So much.' (Carrie, 4a)

'Yeah, I love her to pieces. I wouldn't put up with her otherwise (laughs).' (Niall, 5a)

'I can't imagine being in a relationship with someone I didn't love.' (Sara, 10a)

'Trust me, I wouldn't wash his socks if I didn't love him.' (Chloe, 9a)

'Ultimately it's the one thing that you can't compromise on, you have to have love.' (Jeff, 7b)

The remaining interviewees were equally unhesitant in their answers of 'yes', or 'of course', with little hesitation or reflection. Older respondents echoed this:

'Of course.' (Fiona, 21a)

'I wouldn't have married her otherwise.' (Trevor, 21b)

'Oh yes, I love him just as much now as the day we married, if not more.' (Marie, 22a)

'Absolutely.' (Anton, 22b)

'Oh, I love him to bits.' (Anne, 23a)

'She's the love of my life.' (Patrick. 23b)

'Oh yes, in spite of all his faults.' (Liz, 24a)

'Well, he's my husband.' (Barbara, 25a)

'Oh yes.' (Richard, 25b)

In many of these responses the 'one and only' ideal of romantic love is alluded to, for example in Patrick's assertion that Ann is the love of his life. This jars with the contemporary ideal of confluent love, as does Liz's description of loving her husband in spite of his faults. Within a pure relationship partners should not be a burden upon one another. Several of the younger respondents also describe loving their partners in these terms, as Chloe laughs about love being the reason she washes her partner's socks. For both generations of respondents love is seen to involve self-sacrifice and an element of practical care. My interviewees were more reticent when questioned about the meaning of love, with the majority of both generations of respondents describing it as a 'feeling' that is difficult to verbalize, but that is felt intuitively:

'I don't know, it's when you really care about someone, but it's more than that.' (Paul, 9b)

'It's hard to explain, you just know.' (Steven, 10b)

'It's not something you can put into words.' (Dawn, 7a)

'When you just love someone, it's a feeling you have.' (Emma, 11a)

'You don't really have to describe it, it's something you feel.' (Ali, 6a)

'What kind of question's that? I'm not very good with words.' (Marie, 22a)

'You know inside.' (Patrick, 23b)

The respondents refer to love as a presocial emotion that is lessened by being put into words. Several respondents also make the distinction between the initial stage of falling in love and loving someone in the long term:

'You start off in that infatuation stage, then it tails off so you just love that person.' (Paul, 9b)

'You don't feel as passionate after a while, but you love them more, if you know what I mean.' (Carrie, 4a)

'It's more intense at first, but I think it means more after a couple of years.' (John, 4b)

'Well, we're not like kids anymore, but I wouldn't be without him.' (Fiona, 21a)

'When you've been together for this long, you can't imagine life without the other person.' (Liz, 24a)

Although gender differences in describing communication were marked, there was remarkably little discrepancy between male and female descriptions of love, and nothing to indicate that it was more important to one that the other. While the need for emotional disclosure was described by both genders as being more important to women, love is something both partners find essential and claim to experience. Women may be more skilled at 'doing' intimacy; however I have found no evidence to suggest that they experience it on a deeper level to their partners. Of particular interest was the dialogue between the male participants in the focus group:

How do you define love?

A – I guess not expecting it, it just happens.

S – It's a good question.

C– It's one of these things, love, isn't it.

P – That's what's beautiful about it.

S – Yeah, it's a feeling, it's not anything solid.

A – It means different things to different people.

S – You look at Shakespeare's stuff, and he wrote about love, but I'm sure if you asked him to define it he couldn't, it's just how people feel, how people are, I don't think you can nail it down to "I feel like this".

(Male focus group, 20–35)

The participants debate the meaning of love, coming to the conclusion that it is in essence indefinable. Although romance is often understood to mean more to women, the men in the group display an understanding of the discourses surrounding love and make references to Shakespeare and the 'beauty' of love. They go on to discuss personal experiences of love, and unlike the interview respondents, openly question their feelings:

P – A lot of people don't think about it enough, perhaps, you assume you are. I reckon a lot of people who think they're in love really aren't, have some misgivings, maybe I'm one of those people.

S – Towards the end of my previous relationship I was thinking do I love her? Perhaps I do, perhaps I don't. People say you should just know, and if you don't, then you aren't, there's no asking yourself. If you are asking yourself, you aren't. At the time, it cemented my knowledge that things weren't good.

P – I think you can just get comfortable.

C – That's definitely how my relationship was – I was like actually am I really in love with this person? Do I actually see myself with them in twenty years' time? Do I actually want to go any further?

P – I remember the first girl I went out with for a long period of time, I was sure I was in love with her, and she's still one of my best friends, so there's obviously something there, the thing that gutted me was not being with her family anymore, you're in such a comfort zone.

A – Yeah, some people don't like to start again, it's scary, you've got to go out there and find someone, and do the whole thing all over again, it's easier to settle.

P – When you're in the comfort zone there's almost no effort involved in the relationship, you take each other for granted.

A – But relationships can't always be at that infatuation stage, that doesn't last.

S – Definitely.

A – It'll always tail off, but some relationships will tail off more than others.

P- It's more important for you both to be in a relationship and enjoying it, than for you to be going round telling everyone that you're madly in love.

S – I guess what you're saying is that it's fine to be in a relationship if you're both happy, so you shouldn't therefore sack it off and go looking for love, you should stick with what you've got, is that what you're saying?

A – Unless you're unhappy, then fair enough.

P – I'm not saying this is my beliefs, of what I want to do in my life, I'm saying I can see why people stay in loveless marriages, relationships, yet both really enjoying it. I don't think I will do that, but I can understand how that might happen.

B – You know you can love people and not enjoy loving them, to the other end of the scale.

(Male focus group, 20–35)

Here the male participants willingly talk about love, and their thoughts and fears on this subject, contradicting the popular belief that women think more deeply about relationships. The focus group provided a safe environment in which the men were able to express themselves, however, there is always an awareness of the other men in the group and in this case as they were all supporting each other's viewpoints the participants were able to speak. The popular romantic ideal of love and its presentation in popular films and television programmes is illustrated in the ways that the men attempt to define love, for example, 'not expecting it, it just happens' (A); 'people say you should just know' (S); 'It's a feeling, it's not anything solid' (S). Rather than doubting the importance of love because of its elusive meaning, the men see this as part of its attraction; 'That's what's beautiful about it' (P). The similarities in the respondents' descriptions of love suggest the importance of cultural understandings of love. However, the respondents are unanimous in their belief that love is an innate emotion that cannot be accurately described.

There was also an awareness of the weight that the ideal of love can place on a relationship, with P's assertion; 'It's more important for you both to be in a relationship and enjoying it, than for you to be going round telling everyone that you're madly in love.' The expectations that the respondents have of finding 'true love' place a huge weight on their relationships (Evans, 2003). Evans is highly critical of modern notions of love, as she insists that while romantic love was initially a form of emancipation, which allowed women to have some say over their marriage partner in the nineteenth century, contemporary discourse has shifted love from an ideal to an expectation. These findings support this, as love seems to be the one aspect of their relationships that the participants are unwilling to compromise on. However, as all of the couples insist that they are in love, it may be that this is an aspect of the couples' management of their image to outsiders. As Evans writes, 'part of our contemporary performance of gender is the performance of the lover or the loved, in appropriately gendered ways' (Evans, 2003: 13).

Summary

The data presented here supports the conclusions drawn by Duncombe and Marsden from their own research, namely that women tend to attach more importance to intimacy and communication than men, and that women are more able to disclose emotionally and 'do' intimacy. Many of the women in the younger sample complained that their partners did not take emotional communication as seriously as they did and that men were generally less able to talk openly about their feelings. Similarly male respondents said that they felt pressured into talking by their partners, while some men expressed frustration at being unable to express their emotions easily. Popular stereotypes of women as emotional and men as rational underpin the respondents' discussions. However, love is described in equal terms by both generations and genders, in that all regard it as crucial to their relationships. I would argue that this does not indicate that love is a transcendent, timeless emotion, rather it suggests that to admit that you do not love your partner passionately but are content within your relationship is socially unacceptable for western individuals of all ages and genders. In this way love exists discursively and is a dominant ideal for the respondents.

Communication is seen as a female responsibility by the couples, supporting Giddens' theory that the shift towards pure relationship is female driven. This would also suggest that women take on the responsibility for maintaining the emotional health of their relationships, which is an unacknowledged area of emotional labour. However, not all emotional labour is carried out by women. Hochschild (1976) argued that emotion work is carried out by actors constantly, including within interviews and focus groups which are social interactions in themselves. For example one of the male participants (Sam) was overcome with emotion in the interview and began to cry. This contrasted starkly with his behavior in the focus group, where he joined in with the raucous discussion of

128

the other men. This provides an illustration of Hochschild's point that emotions are regulated according to the perceived appropriateness of the situation an actor finds him or herself in.

Emotional labour is not always gender specific, as while women encourage their partners to talk about their feelings more, men may perform their own work by withholding their own emotions for fear of compromising their masculinity. Within heterosexual relationships, emotions and roles become specialized, as the male partner may take the role of being independent and strong, while the female partner's role involves her being weak and emotional (Hollway, 1996: 98). Constructing the memory of a relationship may also involve emotional labour, as couples strive to fit their recollections with the present image they wish to promote or believe. This does not always work to support a positive view. For example Liz, an older respondent, laments the lack of affection shown to her by her husband, and supports her complaint by suggesting that he has always been like this:

'I suppose that's what you expect after twenty-five years, you can't expect someone to change.' (Liz, 24b)

Overall, older couples appeared to be less influenced by the modern ideal of constant communication, although there is an acknowledgement that communication is more important to couples of their generation than it was to their parents':

'But my mum and dad, well they never seemed to talk at all, you know it wasn't done in those days.' (Fiona, 21a)

Intimacy is also not confined to verbal communication for the older respondents:

'I don't suppose we talk about our feelings that much, because when you've been together so long you know what the other is thinking, really.' (Anne, 23a)

While Anne and Patrick's relationship may not conform to the ideal of disclosing intimacy they appear to be close and happy with each other. Privileging one type of intimacy over another devalues relationships which do not conform to this ideal. Jamieson (1998) writes that mutual disclosure is not crucial to a good relationship as couples may express affection in other ways and suggests that there are multiple 'practices of intimacy ... which enable, generate and sustain a subjective sense of closeness and being attuned and special to each other' (Jamieson, 2011: 2.1).

It is worth questioning what communication actually achieves. In terms of housework couples often talk about their roles, although this rarely achieves change, and is meaningless unless accompanied by practical action. One female respondent expressed her frustration that talking does not always result in action:

> 'We talk about housework, and he knows my feelings, but it doesn't actually change his behaviour.' (Ali, 6a)

Vogler (2000) posits that the late modern ideal may actually be harmful. She suggests that the 'self-expressive intimacy', which is promoted in self-help literature and is seen as the key to good relationships, can actually have a negative effect and destroy the type of intimacy couples actually want. Vogler (2000: 51) describes the (mainly female) consumers of pop psychology as 'heterosexuality's moral proletariat', charged with producing exemplary heterosexual intimacy at home, which I would argue, results in increased levels of emotional labour. Vogler concludes that the spiritual underpinnings of popular psychology (which Giddens uses as evidence of the pure relationship) are deeply heteronormative in their promotion of egalitarian coupling and their focus on the family as what informs people's sense of self and marks the horizon of their life expectations. Similarly, Evans (2003) urges women to abandon expectations of love, which she argues are individualistic, demanding and commodified and trap women in the domestic contract. With regard to my female respondents, being in a heterosexual relationship undoubtedly demands much domestic and emotional labour, with apparently few returns, which are excused because the couples are 'in love'. Inequalities will persist for as long as heterosexual romance continues to be accepted as women's greatest 'adventure, duty and fulfillment' (Rich, 1989: 654). Jonasdottir (1994) emphasizes the fundamental role of love in reproducing male power. She posits that 'love power' (Jonasdottir 1994: 88) is primarily acted out in personal relationships and translates into women becoming the loving caretakers of men rather than equals within heterosexual relationships, which can be seen in Chloe's explanation, 'I wouldn't wash his socks if I didn't love him.'

Chapter 7
Buying into It: Self-development, Lifestyle and Consumption

One of the most debated aspects of the posited transformation of intimacy is the idea that our intimate relationships are key sites for our self-development. In this chapter I consider the influence of consumer culture and lifestyle on the participants' constructions of their relationships and the role of their relationships in helping them manage their sense of self. The extent to which the older generation studied has embraced a period of 'midlifestyle' (Featherstone and Hepworth, 1991) is also discussed. The importance of consumption in achieving the types of relationships that my respondents aspire to is addressed, with reference to Evans' (2002) discussion of modern love as commercialized.

Reflexivity, Risk and the Project of the Self

Giddens (1991, 1992) and Beck (1992) argue that we live in a post traditional society, in which secure orders of values and social positions have been replaced with a bewildering diversity of values, roles and authorities. Within this context, the concept of risk as an organizing principle of everyday life comes to the fore as fundamental to individual's organization of the social world. Put simply, late modernity is a risk culture, or 'risk society' (Beck, 1992). The uncertainties of the modern world, for example environmental issues, the possibility of apocalyptic warfare and the terrorism threat, have resulted in risk becoming an unavoidable part of our contemporary experience (Giddens, 1991: 3, 4). Within a risk society, intimate relationships achieve a heightened importance as an anchor for self-development, yet the fragility of modern relationships paradoxically contributes to the sense of risk underlying everyday life.

Within the context of a risk society, theorists such as Beck and Giddens posit that self-identity must be reflexively organised. It becomes established through a process of sustaining coherent yet continuously revised biographical narratives. As a result of 'reflexive modernisation' (Beck, 1994) biography, which was once restricted by traditional guidelines, becomes 'elective' (Beck and Beck-Gernsheim, 1995: 25). The notion of lifestyle takes on particular significance within this context. For Giddens (1991), lifestyle gives material form to a particular narrative of self-identity. Exclusive to late modern societies, lifestyles constitute a modern form of social identity, and can be defined as 'patterns of action that differentiate people' (Chaney, 1996: 4). Chaney maintains that lifestyles represent a shift from the importance of production to consumption in the formation of an individual's social identity, as what we buy has become more important to our social status than what we do. Consumer culture connects with self-reflexivity and lifestyle in a number of ways, as individuals use products to construct and display who they are. Baudrillard (1988) argued that under postmodernity the nature of consumption has fundamentally shifted, as commodities move from being utilitarian objects to signs and symbols; 'Consumption, in so far as it is meaningful, is a systematic act of the manipulation of signs' (Baudrillard, 1988: 22).

Lifestyles are the product of 'habitus', a term which Bourdieu (1977) used to describe the mechanism through which an individual's actions become an embodied product of his or her conditioned perception of the world. The habitus represents the existential environment of an individual, including beliefs and tastes, and prefigures the choices that that individual makes. Choices are therefore not limitless as although there may be countless options available, they only exist as realistic possibilities to the extent that an individual considers them so. While individuals may enjoy an element of flexibility, the concept of the habitus denies complete agency. Although Bourdieu regarded his analysis as reflexive, a critique is that his view is overly deterministic (Chaney, 1996: 66). While Giddens posits lifestyle choices as available to all regardless of social class, ethnicity and gender, Bourdieu believed that the symbolic mastery necessary to make lifestyle choices is privileged by culturally dominant groups as 'academic qualifications are to cultural capital what money is to economic capital' (Bourdieu, 1977: 187). Bourdieu described the importance of taste as 'a symbolic expression of class position' (Bourdieu, 1984: 175). It is reasonable to expect that the most privileged groups in society will be more able to mobilize lifestyle choices, particularly with the importance of consumption, and therefore money, in establishing and communicating that lifestyle.

Intimate relationships achieve a heightened importance within this context, as they become an area in which the 'narrative of the self' (Giddens, 1991: 54) is grounded. This is because intimacy is often bracketed with authenticity, and a truer version of the self which exists beyond the veneer of consumerism. Giddens' theory is that as individuals are forced to construct their own self-identity, they are able to choose the kinds of lifestyles that they want to lead and, he posits, as a result they increasingly choose relationships based on the principles of democracy and equality. The concept of choice here is problematic, as it can be read to mean free choice rather than, in more sociological terms, contextual choice amongst socially constructed options, as represented by the habitus. In sociological terms there is a very significant difference between the concepts of free choice and contextual choice (Shipman and Smart, 2004).

Beck and Beck-Gernsheim (1995; 2002) share Giddens' assertion that late modernity represents a radical departure from traditional society and maintain that intimate relationships take on a new relevance within this context. The late modern processes of individualization, detraditionalization and increased self-reflexivity are transforming expectations of heterosexual relationships, as 'the ethic of individual self-fulfilment and achievement is the most powerful current in modern society' (Beck and Beck-Gernsheim 2002: 22). It is within this context that 'love, in all its glory ... will turn out to be one of the main sources of satisfaction in personal life' (Beck and Beck-Gernsheim, 1995: 169). Here love is seen as our solution to doubt as although it is high risk the potential for reward is similarly great. The faith placed in love is regarded as an entirely modern phenomenon as it is only now that personal relationships are justified along emotional rather than traditional or formal lines. For individuals who have to invent their own social settings love becomes the central focus of life and is thus elevated to the rank of 'a latter day religion' (Beck and Beck-Gernsheim, 1995: 170). It could be argued that the major shortcoming of both Giddens' and Beck and Beck-Gernsheim's analyses is their lack of direct empirical evidence. While their work is based on late-modern social phenomena such as high divorce rates, the proliferation of self-help literature and the prominence of environmental issues it is problematic to assume that this reflects everyday social reality (Shumway, 2003; Jamieson, 1998). The idea that there has been a sudden and unprecedented shift from 'traditional' marriage has also been disputed (Jamieson, 1998; Gross, 2005; Smart, 2007). Nevertheless, the idea that contemporary relationships represent a radical break with tradition and that 'today's marriage rituals are less about creating social relations than constructing personal identities' (Gillis, 1999: 52) is pervasive within both popular and sociological understanding.

Self-development within Relationships

Love as a solution to doubt is a central tenet of Beck and Beck-Gernsheim's (1995) understanding and the role of relationships as a haven or refuge emerged as a theme within the interviews for both genders of the younger generation of respondents. Although I did not directly question my interviewees about this, many of the comments they made alluded to their relationships as an escape from public life:

> 'It's so nice to have someone to come home to, when you're all stressed from work and stuff.' (Christie, 5a)

'It's like, you know there's always going to be someone on your side, if anything bad happens.' (Paul, 9b)

'I love going out with my mates, but it's different, with a relationship there's always someone there for you.' (Alex, 12b)

'Sometimes you get that cosy you and me against the world feeling, which makes you feel quite close.' (Sara, 10a)

'I wouldn't like to be single, just because you feel quite isolated.' (Teresa, 12a)

This can be seen as evidence for Beck and Beck-Gernsheim's (1995) argument and can be interpreted either as a positive shift, or as a desperate reaction against anomie as is Bauman's (1995) understanding. The respondents quoted here allude to the 'outside world' as a potentially threatening area from which their intimate relationships shield them, for example Christie regards her relationship as an escape from her professional life. The couple relationship is also elevated above other relationships, as Alex describes his relationship with his girlfriend as different from that with his 'mates', as she is always there for him. Similarly Teresa explains that as a single woman she would feel 'isolated'. While friendships are often referred to as an important part of my respondent's lives the couple relationship is afforded a special status. Being in a relationship is seen as a protection against the more threatening aspects of life and as such could be understood to be the most secure arena in which to develop a narrative of the self.

When I questioned the respondents on whether they felt that being in a relationship had encouraged their self-development the responses differed largely according to gender. Many of the younger women questioned felt that being in a relationship gave them the ontological security to develop their self-identities, whereas a number of the men questioned expressed a concern that having a partner limited their personal freedom and experiences.

'A bit of both, really, like I'm more confident now, in social situations, and it's nice to have the security, but, like I was saying, you kind of lose your individuality to some extent.' (Carrie, 4a)

'I think I like the companionship. I guess it's confidence as well, that you tend to be a bit more outgoing. Security too.' (Anna, 3a)

'Oh, helped, definitely. I think I'm quite cynical and negative, and I've taken some of his positivity, but then he's also taken some scepticism from me. And socially, because everyone loves Ian, so we go out more and I feel more confident with him. It sounds really crap, but just being able to show I'm able to get a boyfriend, I have someone who loves me, so totally, it makes me more chilled.' (Jane, 1a)

'No, it's encouraged me. I've changed my outlook. Jeff has just brought so much to my life, I'm more open now, more sociable. I think it's made me a better person.' (Dawn, 7a)

'Being in a relationship gives you more confidence in other areas, I think, like socially and professionally.' (Emma, 11a)

'No, it's helped. It's like it reassures you, raises your self-esteem in a way, even though you might have less independence than when you're single.' (Ali, 6a)

Although Ali and Carrie concede that being in a relationship may compromise their independence, the confidence and self-esteem gained are understood to be worth this sacrifice. The extracts above show an almost universal appreciation of having a boyfriend as a boost in confidence and security for the women interviewed. Dawn eulogizes about being with her partner as having made her a 'better person', and other respondents hint at similar feelings.

Much of the confidence gained appears to be social, with many of the interviewees describing how they feel more comfortable in social situations when accompanied by a partner. The responses to this question garnered positive responses in comparison to the questions about housework, suggesting that this may be one of the reasons why women seek out and maintain heterosexual relationships. While a good relationship can improve a woman's sense of self-esteem, a failing relationship may undermine her confidence:

'He used to make me feel good about myself, but with things going badly I really feel that my confidence has been knocked, and I don't feel that he finds me attractive or respects me. It makes me stressed, and even makes my IBS worse.' (Kate, 2a)

Kate describes how her relationship has affected her physically and emotionally and her testimony highlights the risk that many women take by defining themselves through their relationships and relying on their partners for a sense of security and self-esteem. The body as a reflexive project (Giddens, 1991) may also translate into additional pressure for women to maintain their appearance, as Kate described feeling depressed about the weight she had gained since entering her relationship.

Two of the younger male interviewees also describe how being in a relationship has improved their sense of self-identity:

'I think it helped a lot, because I'm not very assertive, I would still be at home, I would never have left my job, or bought a house, because I wasn't confident enough.' (Sam, 2b)

'Yeah, being in love, it's great. You feel more sure of yourself.' (Alex, 12b)

However, other male respondents did not refer to their relationships as improving their confidence. Many of them described being in a relationship as having held them back in terms of their self-development and the experiences that are open to them:

'It's probably suppressed me, because I don't go out as much, and also because I may have decided to do other things, I mean, I'm young, qualified, on a decent amount of cash, free of debt and I could have gone on a different journey, abroad or somewhere else.' (Jeff, 7b)

'Well, you don't have the freedom, you know to go to the pub, stay out all night or whatever.' (Ben, 6b)

'No, I think if I was single I would be more self-sufficient, you know in a relationship you always have to think of the other person, you don't get to go out as much.' (John, 4b)

'I think my life would be very different, as most of my single friends have been travelling, and when you're in a relationship you can't just go off for a year. So, yeah, I've had to miss out on things.' (Ian, 1b)

'The only thing is you're less independent, so I suppose your self-development would suffer.' (Carl, 3b)

'It's good to be in a relationship, but you are less independent.' (Paul, 9a)

Many of the male respondents frame their relationships as having robbed them of their independence and therefore as having a detrimental effect upon their personal development. In contrast, the younger female respondents describe the sense of security and self-confidence they achieve by having a partner. It would appear that the experiences that the male and female respondents describe are diametrically opposed; while the women endure the burden of physical and emotional labour their pay-off is security and self-esteem. Conversely the men complain about the limits being in a relationship places on their independence, yet benefit from being cared for practically and emotionally by their partners. These findings are indicative of the importance of models of masculinity and femininity (Connell, 1987; 1995) in shaping the attitudes of male and female respondents. While men prioritize independence, or at least recognize the importance of the rhetoric of independence in constructing a heterosexual masculinity, women develop interdependence through their relationships with other people.

Relationships and Lifestyle: Younger Couples

However personal tastes and choices are they fall into distinctive patterns that are associated with other socio-structural characteristics. Intimacy is often seen as distinct from lifestyle, with the self given in intimate settings seen as a truer, more authentic version than that displayed to the world at large. However, evidence from interviews suggests that all of the younger respondents are striving to achieve similar lifestyles based around being in a heterosexual relationship. This suggests the existence of a habitus, or enclosed cultural universe, within which the social group studied here operates:

'We kind of expect the same things anyway. We've not discussed it, said this is our plan, but we both kind of have the same plan in our head, of what we are going to do. Like, when we are going to get married and have children, that sort of stuff.' (Jane, 1a)

'Well, we don't have to talk about it, because we know what we want to do, you know have a nice house, cool stuff to fill the house, expensive holidays, you know 'cause we've both got careers, and we won't have kids for a while. Actually, I would say that we travel, more than go on holidays, as we would never go on a package.' (Ian, 1b)

Ian and Jane acknowledge that they share unspoken goals, which suggests that heterosexual relationships have retained conventional elements, such as having children, as a norm that does not need to be discussed. Other respondents describe the importance of a shared lifestyle to the success of their relationships:

'Well, we do share interests, you know, eating out, drinking, music, we have similar jobs, like our friends really, we all cohabit, but aren't married with kids. It's very similar. I guess that's what keeps us as friends, when people do other things, like go off and have children, you tend to lose touch, don't you?' (Anna, 3a)

'Oh, definitely, drinking, food, films, etc. I guess because we were friends first, but it's stood us in good stead, because after the first year the rush goes, and you actually have to like each other and have things to talk about. We have the same group of friends, and do the same things, so it's cool.' (Carrie, 4a)

'Most mates are like us, you know not married or kids yet, but living together. It's quite weird when someone breaks it, you know, we went to a university friend's wedding a couple of years ago, and everyone was quite sneery because they were getting married so young, and now no one sees them anymore.' (Sara, 10a)

The couples not only share similar lifestyles, which revolve around the consumption of items such as meals out, the cinema, holidays, but also surround themselves with a social group made up of other couples in similar situations and it is important to note the impact that wider networks has on decisions relating to personal relationships (Smart, 2007). Where a couple does not conform to this model as in the case of Sara's friends who married in their early twenties, they are ridiculed and excluded. Single friends may also be excluded because their lifestyles are seen as incompatible with the couples interviewed:

'Yeah, we like to do the same things, and most of our friends are in couples like us. I mean, I do have single friends, but I tend to see them less and less, because we just don't, er, have anything in common anymore.' (Ali, 6a)

'You can feel self-conscious, when you see single people it can be a bit awkward if everyone else is coupled up, you know?' (Dawn, 7a)

The dual income of childless couples in their twenties and early thirties is necessary to support this lifestyle, which would be difficult to maintain as a single person:

'You need to be in a couple to buy a house in your twenties, like us, and all our friends, you know in [exclusive suburb], you both need to be earning a decent wage to afford anything. Single people just can't do it, you know, it's too expensive.' (Sara, 10a)

'It sounds bad, but you know you it makes you put up with stuff, because if you were single, you couldn't, you know, wouldn't be able to afford a house like this on your own, your lifestyle would be very different.' (Anna, 3a)

Anna indicates that advantages of being in a couple outweigh the effort involved in taking care of her home and partner. Starting her sentence with 'I know it sounds bad' suggests that this is not something that should be admitted, as it does not conform to the relationship ideal of love as more important than external factors.

> 'I do miss being single, you know, you can do what you want, don't have to think about anyone else, but if I was, then, I wouldn't have anyone to share the mortgage with, and I wouldn't have spare cash to spend on the home cinema system. Not that that's why I'm in a relationship, but I can see that's why some people stay together (laughs).' (John, 4b)

John initially admits that he is partly in a relationship for the financial benefits it offers, although he is aware that this is not something one 'should' say, and depersonalizes his argument. Cohabiting between two partners with high incomes and no children would give the couple a high disposable income, which enables them to consume products important to their social standing, including expensive televisions, houses and exotic holidays. For many of the couples interviewed the consumption of various activities and objects form a key part of 'doing' intimacy (Duncombe and Marsden, 1993). Evans (2003) argues that marriage now run by the demands of the market, rather than religious authority, and is modelled on standards of convenience, rules, bargains, and efficiency. She argues that contemporary love is commercialized love, as modern partnerships are based on shared tastes, and allegiances to material objects. (Evans, 2003: 136). The lifestyles of the younger couples interviewed here support Evans' claim that the ideal couple within late capitalism is one that can live, dress, consume and travel in ways which accord with the fantasy of consumption.

Bourdieu's theory of class and lifestyle can be employed to explain the tastes and choices of my respondents. Through consumption we display our taste and style; by deciding to live in affluent suburbs and exclusive city centre apartments, my interviewees are making statements about themselves and differentiating themselves from others:

> 'A girl we were friends with in uni went off to live in Rochdale, or somewhere like that, with a plumber she met, God knows why, cause she was a medic.' (Jane, 1a)

Jane displays incomprehension as to why one of her peers would reject the middle class lifestyle displayed by the rest of her social group, which is contingent on choice of partner, as well as the area in which one resides. In this way, choosing a partner also becomes a consumer choice, as another way to display our taste. Taste is not, according to Bourdieu, a matter of individual whim, rather it is socially structured (Slater, 1997: 159), as sets of preferences are socially organized through the habitus. To further explain Bourdieu's complex discussion of the relationship between class and culture, Slater points to the key terms of economic capital and cultural capital. These involve hierarchies of legitimacy, through which certain types of music, for example, are given greater legitimacy than others, with the more powerful groups in society awarding this legitimacy through their endorsement.

Throughout the interviews, many of the respondents inadvertently made comments which revealed their tastes, and therefore their social status, to me. For example, when discussing his holidays, Ian said; 'actually, I would say that we travel, more than go on holidays, as we would never go on a package [holiday].' Similarly, another male respondent spoke of only ever cooking with 'olive oil, never vegetable' (Niall, 5b) in an offhand comment, which again revealed much about his tastes and therefore his social status. I would argue that both the food we eat and our leisure pursuits are signifiers of social class, or more specifically in this case suggest membership of a young professional urban social group.

There is recognition by one respondent that consumerism may have a negative impact upon modern relationships:

> 'We have a lot more money to spend these days, we only think about what makes us happy now. Fifty years ago you couldn't go out and do this, and get pissed, and buy things, that wasn't the life, so you had to have something more, you had to have something else, and relationships are probably part of that. I'm 25, I've got a house, a car, a computer, a DVD player, an X-Box, widescreen TV, and there isn't anything that I couldn't afford now, whereas 50 years ago people lived a lot different, they didn't have money, they had to save, and relationships were a lot more important.' (Sam, 2b)

Sam has had his material needs met in a way that previous generations could only imagine. However, he feels that the instant gratification that he enjoys may come at the expense of emotional development and overshadow the role of his relationship. Sam's concerns are echoed by the detractors of late modernity (Bauman, 1995; Lasch, 1986) who lament the effects of individualization and consumerism upon intimacy.

Modern forms of expertise are provided by the media; television programmes and celebrity culture provide us with examples of what is desirable in a relationship and inform lifestyle choices. As part of the interview, I asked my respondents whether they agreed with this, and in each case I was told that it did not apply to their relationship. However, throughout the course of the interviews the younger respondents made many references to popular television programmes and celebrities, suggesting that the media provides an important reference point for these couples:

> 'I think everyone wants to be like *Cold Feet*, you know, good job, nice house, relationship, and maybe when they're thirty five have kids.' (Jane, 1a)

'I'm the first to admit I'm a bit of a 'Monica', if you like.' (Carrie, 4a)

This is a reference to a character in the popular US sitcom *Friends*, and it is assumed I will understand it without explanation.

'Well, I don't imagine Posh and Becks fight about the housework, you know.' (Niall, 5b)

'I was like 'Samantha', from *SATC*, you know, before I got involved.' (Ali, 6a)

Again, it is assumed that I will understand the reference to the character 'Samantha', which is further illustrated by Ali's reference to *Sex and the City* as 'SATC'. *Sex and the City* has provided an important reference point for many of the women interviewed, perhaps because it deals exclusively with the intimate lives of four women. Although the women in the programme are single, their unrelenting search for a partner is the central theme, and as such does not undermine the relationships that my respondents are in.

'I think if I was single, I'd live the kind of *Sex and the City* life, like casual sex and shopping.' (Jane, 1a)

The female respondents make the majority of references to celebrities and television series, which suggests that they are targeted at women who appear to have the primary responsibility for and interest in maintaining their relationships.

The data suggests that relationships appear to come with a number of expectations and aspirations attached. The participants, perhaps unconsciously, have sought out partners who want the same things, and while this may not be enough to keep partners together, it is the reason for two of the couples to separate during the course of the study, Sam and Kate cite 'not enough in common', while Ben and Ali 'want different things'. Here differences in aspirations are given as primary reasons for a relationship break up, before love and sex. Furthermore, all of the couples studied come from similar backgrounds, in terms of religion, social class, age, ethnicity and their parents' occupations. The individualization thesis posits choosing a partner as a free choice, based on emotional compatibility, rather than external factors such as race and class. However, the respondents here have largely chosen partners who share their cultural background, as well as similar lifestyles, meaning that relationships are not only chosen within the parameters of lifestyle, but also social class, background and ethnicity. This would suggest that it is not only important for individuals from transnational backgrounds to choose partners from within their culture, as Smart and Shipman (2004) posit, but also for the highly educated urban middle-classes from which this sample has been selected. While the couples have made choices to enter and sustain heterosexual relationships I would argue that rather than this being a completely free choice, as Giddens suggests, this is a contextual choice. Gross (2005) argues that detraditionalization is not a straightforward process and distinguishes between 'regulative' and 'meaning-constitutive' traditions (Gross, 2005: 286). While regulative traditions, which operate externally may have lost some hold in western societies, meaning constitutive traditions refer to the cultural meanings that are passed down between generations and provide a framework for structuring personal relationships have retained their influence. Gross's theory would explain the ongoing cultural dominance of the dyadic heterosexual relationship and its desirability in my respondents' eyes.

Relationships and Lifestyle: Older Couples

The cohort represented by the older generation in this study is theoretically within a phase of 'midlifestyle' (Featherstone and Hepworth, 1991), which has more in common with understandings of youth than old age. As this generation no longer has dependent children, increased attention may be focussed upon their marriages and lifestyles in general, which may be found wanting, hence the spike in divorce rates for individuals aged forty-five and over (*Social Trends*, 2002). While in their twenties, this generation may not have had the same reflexivity as they presently do in their fifties and sixties. When questioning my older respondents about their decisions to initially enter heterosexual relationships lifestyle choice is not discussed, as my respondents did not challenge the pressure they felt to marry and have children. Choosing to be a wife and mother could be considered a lifestyle choice. However, as the women interviewed did not feel that they had viable alternatives this would not qualify in the understanding of lifestyle as a choice made as part of the narrative of the self. The younger respondents have also chosen traditional heterosexual coupledom, which suggests that alternative lifestyle choices for example same sex relationships or remaining single are restricted to varying extents for both cohorts. The narrative of romantic love can be seen as an influence here for both generations, as the respondents view finding a partner as a quest and frame their relationships in terms of permanence rather than the 'until further notice' qualities of the pure relationship.

Leisure appears to have increased in importance for older respondents with the departure from home of their dependent children. In many cases they are now able to indulge themselves in a 'middle youth':

'Yeah, it's not just us, it's all our friends too, we go out for drinks, and this summer some of us are going to Madeira together. But then, I've not had a social life like this since before I got married, so we probably deserve it.' (Anne, 24a)

Here, mid-life represents a renewed phase of social activity for Anne, who has spent most of her adult life caring for her children, and is now able to indulge in a social life.

'Well we definitely go on more holidays now, we went skiing this winter, and with the après-ski, it was mainly couples our age, you know, who have the means to have these kinds of holidays and pay six pounds for a drink, you know.' (Patrick, 23b)

'It's so important to relax, Barbara goes to her spas, while I play golf. It's not something we've always done, but as you become successful, and have more leisure time, a social life becomes important.' (Richard, 25b)

Consumption is particularly important to establishing the middle-youth lifestyle, as a generous disposable income is necessary to afford the many holidays, meals and drinks out, and leisure pursuits such as golf. While many of the older respondents come from working class backgrounds, they have all successfully established themselves as part of the new middle class that is characteristic of the baby boomer generation. Lifestyles may succeed each other in the life course, however, there appears to be a 'master narrative' for this generation, which is held to ground and inform successive stages of life course. This supports Mannheim's (1952) description of the historical consciousness experienced by different generations. While in their twenties, the older respondents lived more traditional lives, however, the 'empty nest' stage they are experiencing at the time of my research has encouraged a period of increased reflexivity in their lives, where they are able to indulge in leisure pursuits and reflect on their lifestyles. The generational identity of the older couples is a key factor in influencing the choices they make and lifestyles they enjoy.

As mid-life can be a period for self-reflection, the state of a couple's relationship may come under increased scrutiny. Beck and Beck-Gernsheim (1995) argue that once a couple have established a home, a career and raised children, emotional fulfilment and intimacy take on new relevance. For many women this may involve dealing with feelings of bitterness and disappointment at the state of their marriage. The small number of interviews conducted with older women here did not reflect this, perhaps because the couples were happily married. However, the one respondent whose husband refused to take part in the study, Liz, expressed a certain amount of disappointment at the lack of emotional reciprocity within her marriage. Yet rather than choosing to end the relationship she appears to be resigned to the state of her marriage. In this case increased self-reflexivity has not led to action, possibly because women feel less able to mobilize this reflexivity than men. As Barbara argues, it is not uncommon for older men to leave their wives:

'They think they're secure because they've raised children, and been married for thirty years, but their husbands find someone else.' (Barbara, 25a)

The project of the self extends to our relationship with our physical appearance as 'the body can no longer be taken as fixed – a physiological entity – but has become deeply involved with modernity's reflexivity' (Giddens, 1991: 218). With the body as a site of reflexivity the physical effects of ageing in particular have become something to be resisted. As Shilling (2005) writes, cultural images of ageing in the West are overwhelmingly negative and within this context ageing is to be fought rather than accepted. Featherstone and Hepworth (1991) refer to new models of middle age which are strongly related to the older cohort of participants interviewed for this research. The baby boomer generation has garnered particular attention, partly because of its sheer size, but also because its cultural orientation towards youth and large disposable income has made its members particularly susceptible to consumer goods designed to reverse the physical signs of ageing (Blakie, 1999). Featherstone (1991) maintains that it is the expanding middle classes composed of baby boomers that are affected by this trend as the working classes may not have the available resources. Gender may be a further constraint as women generally have less opportunity to be reflexive than men (McNay, 1999).

The older respondents interviewed take a reflexive view of their bodies and compare themselves with previous generations that took a different attitude to ageing:

'Oh, it's so different for us, we go out with our friends regularly, and take holidays, now the boys are grown up. I remember my mother, at my age seemed so old, because she was always working, and they just didn't have the same income. But then, there's more pressure on women my age to look young, you know, we can't let ourselves go.' (Fiona, 21a)

'In her fifties, I thought of my mother as a pensioner, she acted old, as well as looking it, you know she didn't get her hair coloured, or wear new clothes. I definitely don't feel fifty-five.' (Marie, 22a)

These extracts illustrate the importance of the body as a reflexive project of the self, as the older women strive to look younger. It is not only that they want to appear more youthful, but also that their understanding of age in itself has been challenged. While Fiona and Marie·both recall their mothers looking elderly in their fifties, as they and their contemporaries reach this age it has become almost a second youth. However, this does not necessarily mean freedom, as it is coupled with pressure to maintain their looks and deny the ageing process even though they are menopausal. Within a culture that idealizes youthful femininity, ageing is to be resisted. Barbara's thoughts suggest that for her generation to succumb to the ageing process is to fail:

'Well, women my age absolutely cannot let themselves go, because our husbands are still attractive, and if you do a younger women will step in. I've seen it with several of my friends.' (Barbara, 25a)

Barbara's comments illustrate the limits of reflexivity for older women, and suggest that maintaining one's youthful looks is not necessarily a freedom, as the connection between beauty, femininity and youth is precarious (Mac an Ghaill and Haywood, 2007: 109). Reflexivity of the body is largely framed in terms of gender, as older women feel pressure to maintain their femininity. Female identity is set by male demands and expectations of femininity (Lury, 1996), meaning that middle-aged women may suffer new pressures to appear youthful and sexually attractive, whereas previous generations were able to accept the natural ageing process. Western societies have developed a cultural anxiety over the lives of older women that has focused in particular on their intimate relationships and what is deemed to be appropriate behaviour (Mac an Ghaill and Haywood, 2007). Likewise, older women have to carefully regulate how they present themselves physically, in order to avoid dressing too youthfully and looking like 'mutton dressed as lamb', yet at the same time maintaining their attractiveness (Fairhurst, 1989). Growing older for women can be a particularly traumatic experience as their social value is inextricably linked to youth and beauty. Barbara's' fear of her husband leaving if she 'lets herself go' suggests that the same rules don't apply to men, as the physical signs of ageing may work to enhance male social standing (Mac an Ghaill and Haywood, 2007: 117). However, this pressure does not exist exclusively for women. For the older men interviewed, physical appearance takes on a new relevance as they near retirement:

'I worked so hard, all those years, running the cash and carry, that now it is important to go out on the lash, you know, because I never did it before. I'd say most of our friends were younger than me and Fi, but we look as young as they do. Last week I was in a bar with my friend John, who's forty two, and we asked the waitress "who's younger?", and she said me, definitely. So I feel we can keep up with them.' (Trevor, 21b)

Trevor boasts that he looks more youthful than his significantly younger friend, showing that men may also feel pressure to deny the ageing process, although his insecurity about his chronological age may be linked to the fact that he is due to retire shortly as professional status is particularly important to male social power. Hearn (1995) writes that older men have become an invisible group because once retired they are no longer economically productive within the workplace and are not needed to fulfil their paternal role within the family unit. Furthermore, the signs of ageing are linked to inability to perform sexually, which indicates a failure of masculinity (Mac an Ghaill and Haywood, 2007).

The amount of reflexivity enjoyed by the older respondents does appeared to have increased, perhaps because they are at a point in the lifecourse where they no longer have dependent children, coupled with a high disposable income. However, as Evans (2003) suggests, their marriages are now in a sense commercialized as they are based on expensive leisure pursuits and holidays and maintaining a youthful appearance. Furthermore, the late modern focus on the body as a site of reflexivity has heightened the pressure to resist the signs of ageing for both the older men and women interviewed.

Summary

Within this chapter I have investigated the extent to which my respondents have formed relationships as part of a 'narrative of the self' (Giddens, 1991). While the older generation of respondents displayed little reflexivity in their descriptions of entering their relationships in the 1960s and 70s, their lifestyles have changed with their lifecourse to allow them to capitalize on increased leisure opportunities today. The younger generation of interviewees describe entering their relationships as a reflexive choice, although I would argue that these choices are strongly influenced by the habitus they inhabit, which shapes their choices of food, areas in which to live, holidays to take and, I would argue, partner to begin a relationship with. Once in their relationships, traditional expectations of marriage and children come to the fore, as traditional frameworks for structuring personal relationships retain much of their influence (Gross, 2005). Cultural references to popular television programmes and characters are made frequently by the younger women interviewed, and may contribute to the narratives my respondents use to construct their relationships.

Generational identity appears to be linked to habitus, as the tastes and choices of each generation of respondents may be influenced by the different historical locations they occupy (Mannheim, 1952). Reflexive change forms part of the ideology of the couples interviewed, however, this is tempered by structures of gender, generational identity and social class, which limit and influence the choices my respondents make. Both generations of respondents aspire to Evan's (2003) description of the contemporary relationship ideal in which couples live, dress, consume and travel in certain ways, and are largely successful in this endeavour. However, Evans (2003) writes that accompanying this ideal is increasing evidence of social inequality and exclusion. The popular model of love is unattainable by most, simply because they cannot afford it. Where traditional models of love have been usurped, a commodified version has come to the fore. Within this context relationships appear to be based as much on consumption and lifestyle as they are on disclosing intimacy.

Chapter 8
Conclusion

This book has used qualitative data to interrogate the nature of late modern heterosexual partnerships. Here I briefly summarize the main research findings before going on to reflect on the implications of the data. While the in depth interviews and focus groups generated a wealth of data, the findings have been grouped into overlapping themes of commitment, finances, housework, sex, love and intimacy and lifestyle. The overall picture that emerges is one of increasing expectations of equality which are undermined by the social reality of living in a co-resident heterosexual partnership. The posited transformation of intimacy has influenced the ways in which the couples discursively construct their relationships, yet in terms of lived experience their partnerships continue to be underpinned by traditionally gendered roles. What is clearly evident is the centrality of the dyadic heterosexual relationship to the participants' narrative expectations of their lives. For the participants interviewed here, being part of a couple is almost compulsory, with singleness largely regarded as failure. Writing at a time when sociological debate is focused on the consequences of the detraditionalization and democratization of intimacy, these results support more critical interpretations which emphasize the continuation of traditional inequalities and power structures in contemporary relationships.

The authors of reflexive change celebrate what they consider to be the radicalizing effects of late modern social change. Giddens (1991, 1992) and Beck and Beck-Gernsheim (1995, 2002) document the emergence of a new social order of 'reflexive modernity', which they claim has led to a transformation in the experience of the personal. For Giddens, post-traditional society has liberated men and women from the roles and constraints associated with traditional social ties, leaving them to reflexively create their selves through day-to-day decisions. This reflexivity of the self extends to personal relationships, which are evaluated and conducted from a position of self-awareness. This 'transformation of intimacy' is both a response to and a feature of social change, and is argued to have resulted in the emergence of 'confluent love', the 'pure relationship' and 'plastic sexuality' (Giddens, 1992). Similarly, Beck and Beck-Gernsheim's individualization thesis argues that as industrial society collapses, along with its fixed gender and occupational roles, individuals are forced to search for personal satisfaction. Within this context personal relationships have come to lie at the centre of our detraditionalized lives, although they have to be negotiated and discussed as traditional, inegalitarian relationships become obsolete. Cancian's (1987) earlier work articulates a similar picture with a move towards an androgynous, 'interdependent' ideal, in which the quality of a relationship is more important than its structure.

The gender equality that is a necessary precondition to confluent love is not apparent within my respondents' relationships, as gains in the workplace are undermined by the amount of domestic and emotional labour still carried out by women. Giddens and Beck and Beck-Gernsheim acknowledge that gender equality has not yet been fully realized, but insist that it is underway. While changing expectations do cause some conflict within their relationships, the couples interviewed focus much of their energy on defending and justifying gender inequalities rather than challenging them. Reflexivity is also limited, as although the younger couples describe entering their relationships as a choice, commitment appears to be more characterized by drift on the basis of taken-for-granted assumptions of the direction their relationships will naturally take. The older generation of respondents displayed little reflexivity in their descriptions of entering their relationships in the 1960s and 70s, however, their lifestyles have changed with the lifecourse to allow them to capitalize on increased leisure opportunities today. While reflexive change is an influential discourse for the couples interviewed, this is tempered by structures of gender, generational identity and social class, which limit and influence the choices that they make.

Disclosing intimacy is an important ideal for the younger couples, yet inability to always live up to it caused tension and dissatisfaction. It could also be argued that disclosing intimacy is not as democratizing as authors such as Giddens (1991, 1992) suggest. It has been suggested that the promotion of intimacy as the centre of late modern life is a deeply heteronormative ideal (Vogler, 2000). While heterosexual relationships continue to involve greater female sacrifices of emotional and physical labour we should perhaps not expect them to be the site of gender equality. The older couples appeared to be less influenced by the late modern ideal of disclosing intimacy, although there is an acknowledgement that communication is more important to couples of their generation than it was to their parents. Intimacy is also not confined to verbal communication for the older respondents, who often described experiencing an unspoken awareness of what their partner is thinking as one of the strengths of their relationships. The privileging of disclosing intimacy as more authentic or valid devalues relationships that do not conform to this ideal. Yet, as Jamieson (1998) writes, mutual disclosure is not crucial to a good relationship as couples may express affection in other ways that are no less meaningful.

The findings indicate that wider social understandings of appropriate sexual behaviour have changed, as the younger women interviewed openly described a period of promiscuity before forming their relationships. Yet although heterosexuality has been largely uncoupled from monogamy and reproduction it remains the officially sanctioned 'normal' expression of sex (Hawkes, 1996: 6).

Once in a long term heterosexual relationship the pressure is on the female partner to ensure that her partner is satisfied, as the male sexual drive takes priority. I would argue that intimacy and equality within my respondent's sexual relationships is undermined by their continuing reliance on essentialist understandings of masculinity and femininity, as shifts in the outward forms of heterosexuality have done little to change heterosexual practice and popular belief in the naturalness of sex drives.

This research has found limited evidence to support theories of detraditionalization. The 'meaning-constitutive traditions' identified by Gross (2005: 295), continue to shape couples experiences of their relationships as contemporary heterosexual relationships display many of the gender inequalities that characterized previous generations. Importantly, the relationships studied are not moving in the direction of equality, as couples expend more effort in defending the inequalities within their relationships than in seeking to change them. It appears that the authors of detraditionalized sexualities do not always consider the investments that men and women have with traditional notions of masculinity and femininity (McNay, 1999).

These findings also refute theories that emphasize the breakdown of personal relationships, which are based on the same premise of detraditionalization and individualization employed by the proponents of reflexive change. I uncovered little evidence to suggest that either generation of respondents viewed relationships as 'ready-to-consume' products which are discarded when no longer rewarding, as Bauman (2000) has argued. However, his description of relationships as commodified has some resonance, as for the younger respondents a joint income was important for them to achieve the types of lifestyles that they aspired to. The younger couples are largely successful in their attempts to achieve relationships based on an ideal in which couples live, dress, consume and travel in certain ways. Evans (2003) notes that increasing evidence of social inequality and exclusion accompanies this ideal. The popular model of love is unattainable for most, simply because they cannot afford it. Where traditional models of love based on duty have been usurped, a commodified version has come to the fore. The evidence generated here suggests that contemporary relationships are based as much on consumption and lifestyle as they are on disclosing intimacy.

This book supports a more sceptical approach, which emphasizes the continuities which characterize heterosexual relationships, rather than focussing on posited changes. Although this perspective has not received as much popular or sociological attention as the more dramatic theories of either democratization or breakdown, it is grounded in empirical evidence and acknowledges that notions of individualization and democratization are not fully representative of contemporary family life (Ribbens McCarthy et al., 2003). While emotional and domestic labour remain largely female responsibilities, it cannot be assumed that lived heterosexual relationships are gradually moving towards an egalitarian ideal. Feminist theorists (Smart and Shipman, 2004; Stacey, 1996) have argued that only certain groups in society are able to capitalize on late modern discourses of equality. However, the evidence presented here suggests that even dual-career, childless, middle-class couples have failed to realize many of the possibilities described. Lived heterosexual relationships reflect late modern ideals in limited ways, as although small increases in men's participation in domestic labour and food preparation have been detected, the emergence of an egalitarian, androgynous 'pure' relationship appears to be profoundly overstated. Jamieson maintains that public stories have changed more dramatically than private practices, and although people draw on public stories to make sense of their own lives, the two do not provide neat reflections of each other (Jamieson, 1998: 158).

The ideological underpinnings of the two dominant perspectives may be one reason for their overstatement. Theorists promoting individualization and detraditionalization as offering equality in intimate relations generate a view of democracy and justice that operates independently from wider structural constraints (Gillies, 2003: 16). For these theorists the democratization of the family is hailed as a private, personal transformation, occurring regardless of the inequity and discrimination which characterizes the public sphere. Alternatively, those who stress the breakdown caused by late modern social processes tend to endorse a conservative agenda promoting values of responsibility and duty at the expense of social and economic inequities. As Smart and Shipman (2004) write, the individualization thesis can quickly slide from sociological analysis to a moral rant. While this book is aligned with theories of continuity, it is possible that in challenging the detraditionalization thesis advocates of this perspective may overlook evidence of social change. For this reason I would argue for the need of a sociological analysis based on grounded, empirical research rather than political ideologies and for a move away from the three, entrenched positions.

As is often the case with sociological research, this study has raised as many questions as it has answered. Providing an empirical exploration of the debate on intimacy was always an ambitious aim and lack of space has meant that certain issues have not been granted the attention that they merited. Difficulties in recruiting older respondents, perhaps because of the sensitive nature of the research, resulted in a greater focus on the accounts of the larger sample of younger couples. However, the accounts of the older respondents point to the importance of further research into the relevance of the lifecourse in shaping expectations and experiences and to the value of inter-generational research.

The data generated by the focus groups was copious, yet was used only to supplement the accounts of the interviewees. However, the revealing interactions between the focus group participants indicated the importance of developing this approach as a qualitative sociological research method in its own right rather than as an add-on to more established methods. With regard to the interviews, the research was conducted using many of the techniques and insights developed by oral historians. This approach led to a focus on the respondents' memories and feelings and the narratives they used to construct their own experiences. This was particularly compatible with my social constructionist background, and leads me to argue for a greater use of oral history methodologies within qualitative sociological research. The qualitative nature of my research led away from making generalizations and emphasizzed the distinctions within my respondents' accounts. However, analysis of the evidence generated led to the emergence of certain themes and patterns, which support the claims made within this thesis.

This book was deliberately focused on a small number of affluent heterosexual couples whose accounts are inevitably partial and socially situated. While the reasons for this are valid, as I wanted to problematize heterosexualities and focus on the accounts of couples most likely to be affected by the posited changes in personal relationships, it has led to a particularly narrow focus. Future research should perhaps focus on the experiences of more marginalized groups in society, with further exploration of the ways in which generation, ethnicity, social class, sexuality and age affect experiences and expectations of relationships.

The evidence presented here suggests that while there have been changes in the outward forms of heterosexual relationships, with a dual-earner model now the norm and most couples engaging in an extended period of cohabitation before committing to marriage, these partnerships continue to be characterized by gender inequalities. Discourses of equality provide only a partial picture, as younger couples work to maintain relationships based on traditional notions of gender rather than seeking to challenge them. While heterosexuality continues to be based on the socially constructed differences, rather than the similarities between men and women, discourses of equality have little hope of realization.

References

Adkins, L. 1999. Community and Economy: A Retraditionalization of Gender? *Theory, Culture and Society*, 16(1), 117–37.

Albury, K. 2002. *Yes Means Yes: Getting Explicit About Heterosex*. Sydney: Allen and Unwin.

Anderson, E. 2012. *The Monogamy Gap: Men, Love, and the Reality of Cheating*. New York: Oxford University Press.

Arber, S. and Ginn, J. 1995. The mirage of gender equality: Occupational success in the labour market and within marriage. *British Journal of Sociology*, 46(1), 21–43.

Badinter, E. 1995. *XY: On Masculine Identity*. New York: Columbia University Press.

Barker, M and Langdridge, D. 2010. Whatever happened to non-monogamies? Critical reflections on recent research and theory. *Sexualities*, 13(6), 748–72.

Barlow, A., Duncan, S., James, G. and Park, A. 2005. *Cohabitation, Marriage and the Law: Social Change and Legal Reform in the 21st Century*. Oxford: Hart Publishing.

Barnes, H. and Parry, J. 2003. *Renegotiating Identity and Relationships: Men's and Women's Adjustments to Retirement*. Policy Studies Institute, University of Westminster: PSI Report No. 892.

Barnes, J.A. 1979. *Who Should Know What? Social Science, Privacy and Ethics*. Cambridge: Cambridge University Press.

Baudrillard, J. 1988. *America*. London: Verso.

Bauman, Z. 1987. *Legislators and Interpreters: On Modernity, Postmodernity and Intellectuals*. Cambridge: Polity Press.

Bauman, Z. 1998. On Postmodern Uses of Sex. *Theory, Culture and Society*, 15 (3–4), 19–33.

Bauman, Z. 1995. The Making and Unmaking of Strangers. Reprinted in *The Bauman Reader*, edited by P. Beilharz . Oxford: Blackwell, 200–17.

Bauman, Z. 2000. *Liquid Modernity*. Cambridge: Polity Press.

Baxter, J. 2000. The joys and justice of housework. *Sociology*, 34(4), 609–31.

Beagan, B., Chapman, G.E., DSylva, A. and Basset, B.R. 2008. It's just easier for me to do it: rationalizing the family division of foodwork. *Sociology*, 42(4), 653–71.

Beall, A.E. and Sternberg, R.J. 1995. The social construction of love. *Journal of Social and Personal Relationships*, 12(3), 417–38.

Beck, U. 1992. *Risk Society*. London: Sage.

Beck, U. and Beck-Gernsheim, E. 2002. *Individualization*. London: Sage.

Beck, U. and Beck-Gernsheim, E. 1995. *The Normal Chaos of Love*. Cambridge: Polity Press.

Beck, U., Giddens, A. and Lash, S. 1994. *Reflexive Modernization: Politics, Tradition and Aesthetics in the Modern Social Order*. Cambridge: Polity.

Blackie, A. 1999. *Ageing and Popular Culture*. London: Sage.

Blasius, M. 1994. *Gay and Lesbian Politics: Sexuality and the Emergence of a New Ethic*. Philadelphia: Temple University Press.

Bittman, M. and Lovejoy, F. 1993. Domestic Power: Negotiating an Unequal Division of Labour Within a Framework of Equality. *Australian and New Zealand Journal of Sociology*, 29(3), 302–21.

Blumberg, R.L. and Tolbert Coleman, M. 1989. A Theoretical Look at the Gender Balance of Power in the American Couple. *Journal of Family Issues*, 10(2), 225–50.

Bourdieu, P. 1977. *Outline of a Theory of Practice*. Cambridge: Cambridge University Press.

Bourdieu, P. 1984. *Distinction: A Social Critique of the Judgement of Taste*. Cambridge. Massachusetts: Harvard University Press.

Bradley, H. 2007. *Gender*. Cambridge: Polity Press.

Brannen, J. and Moss, P. 1991. *Managing Mothers: Dual Earner Households After Maternity Leave*. London: Unwin Hyman.

Breeze, M. 2009. *Analyzing Young Women's Experiences of Hidden Gendered Power in Heterosexual Relationships*. Edinburgh Working Papers in Sociology No. 33, Edinburgh: University of Edinburgh.

Butler, J. 1990. *Gender Trouble: Feminism and the Subversion of Identity*. London: Routledge.

Cancian, F.M. 1987. *Love in America*. Cambridge: Cambridge University Press.

Caplan, J. 2009. Cheating 2.0: New Mobile Apps Make Adultery Easier. *Time Magazine* [online] 29/6/2009, available at http://www.time.com/time/magazine/article/0,9171,1909602,00.html [accessed on 15/3/12].

Carabine, J. 1996. Heterosexuality and social policy. In *Theorising Heterosexuality*, edited by D. Richardson. Buckingham: Open University Press, 55–75.

Carter, J. 2010. *Why Marry? Young Women Talk about Relationships, Marriage and Love*. PhD Thesis, University of York.

Chaney, D. 1996. *Lifestyles*. London: Routledge.

Chung, D. 2005. Violence, Control, Romance and Gender Equality: Young Women and Heterosexual Relationships. *Womens Studies International Forum*, 28(6), 445–55.

Connell, R.W. 1987. *Gender and Power*. Cambridge: Polity Press.

Connell, R.W. 1995. *Masculinities*. Cambridge: Polity Press.

Craib, I. 1994. *The Importance of Disappointment*. London: Routledge.

Dabhoiwala, F. 2012. *The Origins of Sex: A History of the First Sexual Revolution.* London: Allen Lane.

Dallos, S. and Dallos, R. 1997. *Couples, Sex and Power.* Buckingham: Open University Press.

Dempsey, K. 1998. Men and Womens Power Relationships and the Persisting Inequitable Division of Labour. Paper presented at *Changing Families, Challenging Futures* 6th Australian Institute of Family Studies Conference Melbourne 25–27 November 1998.

Dryden, C. 1998. *Being Married, Doing Gender: A Critical Analysis of Gender Relationships in Marriage.* London: Routledge.

Duncan, S. 2011. Personal Life, Pragmatism and Bricolage. *Sociological Research Online*, 16 (4) 13.

Duncombe, J. and Marsden, D. 1993. Love and Intimacy: The gender division of emotion and emotion work. *Sociology*, 27(2), 221–41.

Duncombe, J. and Marsden, D. 1995. 'Can Men Love': Reading, Staging and Resisting the Romance. In *Romance Revisited*, edited by L. Pearce and J. Stacey. London: Lawrence and Wishart, 238–50.

Dworkin, A. 1988/1996. Biological Supremacy: The World's Most Dangerous and Deadly Idea. In *Feminism and Sexuality, A Reader*, edited by S. Jackson and S. Scott. Edinburgh: Edinburgh University Press, 57–62.

Edley, N. and Wetherall, M. 1995. *Men in Perspective: Practice, Power and Identity.* Hemel Hempstead: Harvester Wheatsheaf.

Eisenstein, H. 1984. *Contemporary Feminist Thought.* London and Sydney: Unwin.

England, P. 2010. The Gender Revolution: Uneven and Stalled. *Gender and Society*, 24(2), 149–66.

Evans, M. 1994. *The Woman Question.* London: Sage.

Evans, M. 2003. *Gender and Social Theory.* Buckingham: Open University Press.

Evans, M. 2003. *Love: An Unromantic Discussion.* Cambridge: Polity Press.

Fairhurst, E. 1989. 'Growing old gracefully' as opposed to 'mutton dressed as lamb': The Social Construction of Recognising Older Women. In *The Body in Everyday Life*, edited by S.J. Nettleton and S.J. Watson. London: Routledge.

Featherstone, M. and Hepworth, M. 1991. The Midlifestyle of George and Lynne. In *The Body: Social Processes and Cultural Theory*, edited by M. Featherstone, M. Hepworth and B. Turner. London: Sage.

Felmlee, D.H. 1994. Who's on Top? Power in Romantic Relationships. *Sex Roles*, 31(5–6), 275–95.

Fielding, H. 1996. *Bridget Jones's Diary.* London: Picador.

Finch, J. 1984. It's Great to Have Someone to Talk to: The Ethics and Politics of Interviewing Women. In *Social Researching: Politics, Problems, Practice*, edited by C. Bell and H. Roberts. London, Routledge & Kegan Paul: 166–80.

Finch, J. and Mason, J. 1993. *Negotiating Family Responsibilities.* London: Routledge.

Finch, J. and Summerfield, P. 1999. Social Reconstruction and the Emergence of Companionate Marriage, 1945–59, in *The Sociology of the Family*, edited by G. Allan. Oxford: Blackwell.

Foucault, M. 1990. *The History of Sexuality: Volume One, An Introduction*. London: Penguin.

Friedan, B. 1965. *The Feminine Mystique*. London: Penguin.

Frith, H. and Kitzinger, C. 1998. 'Emotion Work' as a Participant Resource: A Feminist Analysis of Young Women's Talk-In-Interaction. *Sociology*, 32(2), 299–320.

Furedi, F. 2003. *Therapy Culture: Cultivating Vulnerability in an Uncertain Age*. London: Routledge.

Gabb, J. 2010. Researching Intimacy in Families. Basingstoke: Palgrave Macmillan.

Gavron, H. 1966. *The Captive Wife: Conflicts of Housebound Mothers*. London: Penguin.

Gershuny, J. Godwin. M. and Jones, S. 1994. The Domestic Labour Revolution: A Process of Lagged Adaptaion. In *The Social and Political Economy of the Household*, edited by M. Anderson et al. Oxford: Open University Press.

Giddens, A. 1991. *Modernity and Self-identity*. Cambridge: Polity Press.

Giddens, A. 1992. *The Transformation of Intimacy*, Cambridge: Polity Press.

Giddens, A. 1999. *The Reith Lectures*. http://www.lse.ac.uk/Giddens/reith.htm.

Giddens, A. and Pierson, C. 1998. *Conversations with Anthony Giddens: Making Sense of Modernity*. Cambridge: Polity Press.

Gillies, V. 2003. Family and Intimate Relationships: A Review of the Sociological Research. *Families & Social Capital ESRC Research Group Working Paper No. 2*. London: South Bank University.

Gillis, J. 1985. *For Better, For Worse: British Marriages 1600 to the Present*. Oxford: Oxford University Press.

Gillis, J.R. 1999. 'A Triumph of Hope over Experience': Chance and Choice in the History of Marriage. *International Review of Social History*, 44, 47–54.

Goodnow, J. and Bowes, J. 1994. *Men, Women and Household Work*. Melbourne: Oxford University Press.

Greer, G. 1970/1993. *The Female Eunuch*. London: Flamingo.

Gregson, N. and Lowe, M. 1994. Waged Domestic Labour and the Renegotiation of the Domestic Division of Labour within Dual Career Households. *Sociology*, 28(1), 55–78.

Gross, N. 2005. The Detraditionalization of Intimacy Reconsidered. *Sociological Theory*, 23(3), 286–311.

Hakim, C. 2009. Women's Lifestyle Preferences in the 21st Century. In *The Future of Motherhood in Europe*, edited by J. Schippers, G. Beets and E. te Velde. Dordrecht: Springer.

REFERENCES

Harris, I.M. 1995. *Messages Men Hear: Constructing Masculinities*. London and Bristol: Taylor & Francis.

Hawkes, G. 1996. *A Sociology of Sex and Sexuality*. Buckingham: Open University Press.

Heaphy, B. and Yip, A.K.T. 2003. Uneven Possibilities: Understanding Non-heterosexual Ageing and the Implications of Social Change. *Sociological Research Online*, 8(4).

Hearn, J. 1995. Imaging the ageing of men. In *Born Dying: Images of Ageing*, edited by M. Featherstone and A. Wearnick. London: Routledge.

Heelas, P. 1996. Introduction: Detraditionalization and its Rivals. In *Detraditionalization: Critical Reflections of Authority and Identity*, edited by P. Heelas et al. Oxford: Blackwell, 1–11.

Hendrick, S. and Hendrick, C. 1992. *Romantic Love*. London: Sage.

Hite, S. 2000. *The New Hite Report*. London: Hamlyn.

Hochschild, A. 1976. *The Managed Heart*. Berkeley: University of California Press.

Hochschild, A. 1989. The Second Shift. Viking: New York.

Hockey, J., Robinson, V. and Meah, A. 2004. A heterosexual life: older women and agency within marriage and the family. *Journal of Gender Studies*, 13(3), 227–38.

Hockey, J., Robinson, V. and Meah, A. 2002. For Better or Worse? Heterosexuality Reinvented. *Sociological Research Online*, 7(2).

Hollway, W. 1984/1996. Gender Difference and the Production of Subjectivity, In *Feminism and Sexuality, A Reader*, edited by S. Jackson and S. Scott. Edinburgh: Edinburgh University Press, 84–101.

Hollway, W. 1996. Recognition and heterosexual desire. In *Theorising Heterosexuality*, edited by D. Richardson. Buckingham: Open University Press, 91–109.

Holmes, M. 2004. The Precariousness of Choice in the New Sentimental Order: A Comment on Bawin Legros. *Current Sociology*, 52(2), 251–7.

Irwin, S. 1999. Resourcing the Family: Gendered Claims and Obligations and Issues of Explanation. In *The New Family*, edited by E. Silva and C. Smart. London: Sage, 31–46.

Jackson, S. 1993. Even Sociologists Fall in Love: An Exploration in the Sociology of Emotions. *Sociology*, 27(2), 201–20.

Jackson, S. 1996a. The Social Construction of Female Sexuality. In *Feminism and Sexuality, A Reader*, edited by S. Jackson and S. Scott. Edinburgh: Edinburgh University Press, 62–74.

Jackson, S. 1996b. Heterosexuality, Power and Pleasure. In *Feminism and Sexuality, A Reader*, edited by S. Jackson and S. Scott. Edinburgh: Edinburgh University Press, 175–82.

Jackson, S. 1996c. Heterosexuality and Feminist Theory. In *Theorising Heterosexuality*, edited by D. Richardson. Buckingham: Open University Press, 21–39.

Jackson, S. 2008. Ordinary Sex. *Sexualities*, 11(1/2), 33–37.

Jackson, S. and Scott, S. 2004. Sexual Antinomies in Late Modernity. *Sexualities*, 7(2), 233–48.

Jamieson, L. 1998. *Intimacy: Personal Relationships in Modern Societies*. Cambridge: Polity Press.

Jamieson, L. 1999. Intimacy Transformed? A Critical Look at the Pure Relationship. *Sociology*, 33(3), 477–94.

Jamieson, L. 2011. Intimacy as a Concept: Explaining Social Change in the Context of Globalisation or Another Form of Ethnocentricism? *Sociological Research Online*, 16(4), 15.

Jamieson, L., Anderson, M., McCrone, D., Bechhofer, F., Stewart, R. and Li, Y. 2002. Cohabitation and Commitment: Partnership Plans of Young Men and Women. *Sociological Review*, 50(3), 356–77.

Jamieson, L., Morgan, D.H.J., Crow, G. and Allan, G. 2006. Friends, Neighbours and Distant Partners: Extending or Decentring Family Relationships? *Sociological Research Online*, 11(3).

Jonasdottir, A. 1994. *Why Women are Oppressed*. Philadelphia: Temple University Press.

Jong, E. 1974. *Fear of Flying*. London: Grafton.

Jong, E. 1998. *What Do Women Want? Bread Roses Sex Power*. London: Harper Collins.

Kanneh, K. 1996. Sisters Under the Skin: A Politics of Heterosexuality. In *Feminism and Sexuality, A Reader*, edited by S. Jackson and S. Scott. Edinburgh: Edinburgh University Press, 172–5.

Kemmer, D. 2000. Tradition and Change in Domestic Roles and Food Preparation. *Sociology*, 34(2), 323–3.

Kimmel, M.S. 2001. Masculinity as Homophobia: Fear, Shame and Silence in the Construction of Gender Identity. In *The Masculinities Reader*, edited by S. Whitehead and F. Barrat. Cambridge: Polity Press.

Koedt, A. 1972/1996. The Myth of the Vaginal Orgasm. In *Feminism and Sexuality, A Reader*, edited by S. Jackson and S. Scott. Edinburgh: Edinburgh University Press, 111–17.

Komter, A. 1989. Hidden Power in Marriage. *Gender and Society*, 3(2), 187–216.

Krueger, R.A. and Casey, M.A. 2000. *Focus Groups*. California: Sage.

Langford, W. 1999. *Revolutions of the Heart: Gender, Power and the Delusions of Love*. London: Routledge.

Laqueur, T., 1990. *Making Sex: Body and Gender from the Greeks to Freud*. Massachusetts: Harvard University Press.

Lasch, C. 1986. *The Culture of Narcissism*. London: Abacus.

REFERENCES

Lawson, A. 1989. *Adultery: An Analysis of Love and Betrayal*. Oxford: Blackwell.

Layder, D. 1994. *Understanding Social Theory*. London: Sage.

Lee, R. and Renzetti, C. 1993. The Problems of Researching Sensitive Topics. In *Researching Sensitive Topics*, edited by R. Lee and C.Renzetti. California: Sage, 3–13.

Levy, A. 2005. *Female Chauvinist Pigs: Women and the Rise of Raunch Culture*. New York: Free Press.

Lewis, J. 2001. *The End of Marriage? Individualism and Intimate Relations*. Cheltenham: Edward Elgar Publishing Ltd.

Lewis, J. 2005. Perceptions of Risk in Intimate Relationships. *Journal of Social Policy*, 35(1), 39–58.

Luhmann, N. 1986. *Love as Passion: The Codification of Intimacy*. Cambridge: Polity Press.

Luke, T. 1996. Identity, Meaning and Globalization: Detraditionalization in Postmodern Space Time Compression. In *Detraditionalization: Critical Reflections of Authority and Identity*, edited by P. Heelas et al. Oxford: Blackwell.

Lupton, D. 1999. *Risk*. London: Routledge.

Lury, C. 1996. *Consumer Culture*. London: Routledge.

Mac an Ghaill, M. and Haywood, C. 2007. *Gender, Culture and Society: Contemporary Femininities and Masculinities*. Basingstoke: Palgrave Macmillan.

MacKinnon, C.A. 2002. Pleasure Under Patriarchy. In *Sexuality and Gender*, edited by C.L. Williams and A. Stein. Malden: Blackwell.

Macvarish, J. 2006. What is the Problem of Singleness? *Sociological Research Online*, 11(3).

Mannheim, K. 1952. The Problem of Generations. In *Essays on the Sociology of Knowledge* by K. Mannheim. Routledge and Keegan Paul: London.

Mansfield, P. and Collard, J. 1988. *The Beginning of the Rest of your Life? A Portrait of Newly-wed Marriage*. London: Macmillan.

Mason, J. 1996. *Qualitative Researching*. London: Sage.

Mason, J. 2002. *Qualitative Researching*. London: Sage.

May, T. 1993. *Social Research*. Buckingham: Open University Press.

May, V. 2011. Self, Belonging and Social Change. *Sociology*, 45(3), 363–78.

McMahon, A. 1999. *Taking Care of Men: Sexual Politics in the Public Mind*. Cambridge: Cambridge University Press.

Millet, K. 1970/1989. *Sexual Politics*. London: Virago.

Morgan, D. 1991. Ideologies of Marriage and Family Life. In *Marriage, Domestic Life and Social Change – Writings for Jacqueline Burgoyne 1944–1988*, edited by D. Clark. London: Routledge.

Morgan, D.L. 1997. *Focus Groups as Qualitative Research*. California: Sage.

Morgan, D.L. 1998. *The Focus Group Guidebook*. California: Sage.

Nichols, S. and Metzen, E. 1982. Impact of Wife's Employment upon Husband's Housework. *Journal of Family Issues*, 3, 199–216.

Nowotny, H. 1994. *Time: The Modern and Postmodern Experience*. Cambridge: Polity.

O'Connell Davidson, J. and Layder, D. 1994. *Methods, Sex and Madness*. London: Routledge.

Office for National Statistics. 2011a. *Marriages in England and Wales, 2009*. London: Office for National Statistics.

Office for National Statistics. 2011b. *2011 Annual Survey of Hours and Earnings SOC 2000*. London: Office for National Statistics.

Pahl, R. 1984. *Division of Labour*. Oxford: Blackwell.

Pahl, J. 1989. *Money and Marriage*. Basingstoke: Macmillan Education.

Peggs, K. and Lampard, R. 2000. Irrational Choice: A Multidimensional Approach to Choice and Constraint in Decisions about Marriage, Divorce and Remarriage. In *Rational Choice Theory Resisting Colonisation*, edited by M.S. Archer and J.Q. Tritter. London: Routledge.

Pilcher, J. 1994. Mannheim's Sociology of Generations: An Undervalued Legacy. *British Journal of Sociology*, 45, 481–95.

Pilcher, J. 1995. *Age and Generation in Modern Britain*. Oxford: Oxford University Press.

Plummer, K. 1995. *Telling Sexual Stories: Power, Change and Social Worlds*. London: Routledge.

Plumwood, V. 1993. *Feminism and the Mastery of Nature*. London: Routledge.

Presser, H.B. 1994. Employment Schedules Among Dual-Earner Spouses and the Division of Household Labor by Gender. *American Sociological Review*, 59, 348–64.

Probyn, E. 1993. *Sexing the Self: Gendered Positions in Cultural Studies*. New York: Sage.

Rahman, M. and Jackson, S. 2010. *Gender and Sexuality: Sociological Approaches*. Cambridge: Polity Press.

Ribbens McCarthy, J., Edwards, R. and Gillies, V. 2003. *Making Families: Moral Tales of Parenting and Step-parenting*. London: Sociology Press.

Rieff, P. 1987. *The Triumph of the Therapeutic*. Chicago: The University of Chicago Press.

Reynolds, J. and Wetherall, M. 2003. The Discursive Climate of Singleness: The Consequences for Womens Negotiation of a Single Identity. *Feminism and Psychology*, 13(4), 489–510.

Reynolds, P.D. 1979. *Ethical Dilemmas and Social Science Research*. San Francisco: Jossey-Bass.

Rich, A. 1978/1996. Compulsory Heterosexuality and Lesbian Existence. In *Feminism and Sexuality, A Reader*, edited by S. Jackson and S. Scott. Edinburgh: Edinburgh University Press, 139–44.

Richardson, D. 1996. Heterosexuality and social theory. In *Theorising Heterosexuality*, edited by D. Richardson. Buckingham: Open University Press, 1–21.

Richardson, D. and Monro, S. 2012. *Sexuality, Equality and Diversity*. Basingstoke: Palgrave Macmillan.

Robinson, V. 1996. Heterosexuality and Masculinity: Theorising Male Power or the Male Wounded Psyche? In *Theorising Heterosexuality*, edited by D. Richardson. Buckingham: Open University Press, 109–25.

Robinson, V. 1997. My baby just cares for me: Feminism, Heterosexuality and Non-monogamy. *Journal of Gender Studies*, 6(2), 143–57.

Robson, C. 2002. *Real World Research*. Oxford: Blackwell.

Roseneil, S. 2000. Queer Frameworks and Queer Tendencies: Towards an Understanding of Postmodern Transformations of Sexuality. *Sociological Research Online*, 5(3).

Safilios-Rothschild, C. 1976. A Macro and Micro-Examination of Family Power and Love. *Journal of Marriage and the Family*, 37, 355–62.

Sandfield, A. and Percy, C. 2003. Accounting for Single Status: Heterosexism and Ageism in Heterosexual Women's Talk about Marriage. *Feminism and Psychology*, 13(4), 475–88.

Scott, S. and Jackson, S. 1996. Sexual Skirmishes and Feminist Factions: Twenty-five Years of Debate on Women and Sexuality. In *Feminism and Sexuality, A Reader*, edited by S. Jackson and S. Scott. Edinburgh: Edinburgh University Press, 1–35.

Segal, L. 1987. *Is the Future Female? Troubled Thoughts on Contemporary Feminism*. London: Virago.

Segal, L. 1990. *Slow Motion: Changing Masculinities; Changing Men*. London: Virago.

Sennett, R. 1988. *The Corrosion of Character: The Personal Consequences of Work in New Capitalism*. New York: Norton.

Seymour, J. and Bagguley, P. 1999. *Relating Intimacies: Power and Resistance*. Hampshire: Macmillan.

Shilling, C. 2005. The Rise of the Body and the Development of Sociology. *Sociology*, 39(4), 761–7.

Shumway, D.R. 2003. *Modern Love: Romance, Intimacy, and the Marriage Crisis*. New York: New York Press.

Simmons, C., Kolke, A. and Shimizu, H. 1986. Attitudes Toward Romantic Love Among American, German, and Japanese Students. *Journal of Social Psychology*, 126(3), 327–36.

Sinfield, A. 2004. *On Sexuality and Power*. New York: Columbia University Press.

Smart, C. 1996. Collusion, Collaboration and Confession: On Moving Beyond the Heterosexuality Debate. In *Theorising Heterosexuality*, edited by D. Richardson. Buckingham: Open University Press, 161–78.

Smart, C. 2007. *Personal Life*. Cambridge: Polity Press.

Smart, C. and Shipman, B. 2004. Visions in Monochrome: Families, Marriage and the Individualization Thesis. *British Journal of Sociology*, 55(4), 491–509.

Smart, C. and Stevens, P. 2000. *Cohabitation Breakdown*. London: Family Policy Studies Centre.

Slater, D. 1997. *Consumer Culture and Modernity*. Cambridge: Polity Press.

Stacey, J. 1996. *In the Name of the Family: Rethinking Family Values in the Post Modern Age*. Boston: Beacon Press.

Sullivan, O. 2000. The Division of Domestic Labour: Twenty Years of Change? *Sociology*, 34(3), 437–56.

Sullivan, O. 2004. Changing Gender Practices within the Household: A Theoretical Perspective. *Gender and Society*, 18(2), 207–22.

Sutton, L., Cebulla, A. and Middleton, S. 2003. *Marriage in the 21ˢᵗ Century*, Centre for Research in Social Policy CRSP. Working Paper 482.

Swenson, R. 2009. Domestic Diva? Televised Treatments of Masculinity, Femininity and Food. *Critical Studies in Media Communication*, 26(1), 36–53.

Tichenor, V. 2005. *Earning More and Getting Less: Why Successful Wives Can't Buy Equality*. New Brunswick, NJ: Rutgers University Press.

Tipper, B. 2011. Pets and Personal Life. In *The Sociology of Personal Life*, edited by V. May. London: Palgrave, 85–97.

VanEvery, J. 1996. Heterosexuality and domestic life. In *Theorising Heterosexuality*, edited by D. Richardson. Buckingham: Open University Press, 39–55.

van Gils, W. and Kraaykamp, G. 2008. The Emergence of Dual-Earner Couples: A Longitudinal Study of the Netherlands. *International Sociology*, 23(3), 345–66.

van Hooff, J.H. 2001. *A Qualitative Study of Self-help Manuals*. MA Thesis, University of Manchester.

van Hooff, J.H. 2011. Rationalising Inequality: Heterosexual Couples' Explanations and Justifications for the Division of Housework along Traditionally Gendered Lines. *Journal of Gender Studies*, 20(1), 19–30.

Vogler, C. 2000. Sex and Talk. In *Intimacies*, edited by L. Berlant. Chicago: The University of Chicago Press, 47–83.

Vogler, C., Lyonette, C. and Wiggins R.D. 2008. Money, Power and Spending Decisions in Intimate Relationships. *Sociological Review*, 56(1), 117–43.

Weeks, J. 1995. *Invented Moralities: Sexual Values in an Age of Uncertainty*. Cambridge: Polity Press.

Weeks, J. 2007. *The World We Have Won: The Remaking of Erotic and Intimate Life since 1945*. London: Routledge.

Weeks, J., Heaphy, B. and Donovan, C. 2001. *Same Sex Intimacies: Families of Choice and Other Life Experiments*. London: Routledge.

West, C. and Zimmerman, D. 1987. Doing Gender. *Gender and Society*, 1(2), 125–51.

Whetherell, M. 1995. Romantic Discourse and Feminist Analysis: Interrogating Investment, Power and Desire. In *Feminism and Discourse: Psychological Perspectives*, edited by S. Wilkinson and C. Kitinger. London: Sage.

REFERENCES

Willmott, P. and Young, M. 1975. *The Symmetrical Family: Study of Work and Leisure in the London Region*. London: Penguin.

Wilson, G. 1987. Money: Patterns of Responsibility and Irresponsibility in Marriage. In *Give and Take in Families*, edited by J. Brannen and G. Wilson. London: Allen and Unwin, 136–154.

Wolf, N. 1993. *Fire With Fire: The New Female Power And How It Will Change The 21st Century*. London: Chatto & Windus.

Wyse, J.J., Smock, P.J. and Manning, W.D. 2009. *When She Brings Home the Bacon: Breadwinning and the Sexual-Emotional Lives of Cohabiting Couples*. The Centre for Family and Demographic Research Working Paper Series, http://bgsu.edu/organizations/cfdr.

Young, S. 1998. Is Judith Butler's approach to gender politics an improvement on previous forms of feminism? Available at http://www.theory.org.uk/ctr-b-e1htm.

Index

lifecourse, 82, 146, 150, 152
lifestyle
    and age, 53, 131, 137–147,
      149–152
    and relationship, 11, 15, 22,
      37, 88, 131–132, 137–147,
      149–152
love
    changes in meaning over
      time, 2–8, 12, 16, 18, 50
    definition of, 2–8, 23, 111–113,
      115, 126–129
    expressions of, 42, 44–47, 80,
      103, 114, 122–126, 130
    and sex, 105

male breadwinner model, 55
marriage
    changing attitudes towards, 2, 5,
      7, 11, 16, 18, 30, 37–38, 42,
      47–48, 50, 52–54, 83, 133,
      139, 146
    expectations of, 48–49, 128
Marsden, D., 3, 20–21, 43–44
masculinity, 23, 25–30, 43, 71, 100,
    102, 106, 109, 120–121, 129,
    137, 146, 151
Mason, J., 20, 33
media, 6, 13, 31, 60, 94, 107–108,
    140
methodology, 1, 31, 33, 35, 39, 87,
    93, 111, 114
money
    management of, 55–58, 63,
    and power, 55–56, 58, 61–62,
      64–65
monogamy, 3, 15, 28, 43, 53–54, 99,
    103–104, 150
morality, 8–9, 105, 107
Morgan, D.H.J., 6, 15–16, 25, 29
mortgage arrangements, 42, 46–47,
    53, 56–57, 139
mutual disclosure, 3–5, 18, 20, 111,
    119, 129, 150

narratives, 8, 21, 41, 49, 123, 131,
    146, 153
negotiation, 7, 17, 40, 78–80, 82, 84
'narrative of the self', 3, 13, 112,
    132, 134, 142, 146

ontological security, 134
orgasm, 89

paid help, 77, 78, 84
part-time work, 35, 63
partnership, 1–2, 11, 18–19, 37–38,
    44–45, 54–55, 62, 67–68, 98,
    103–104, 139, 149, 153
patriarchy, 24–27, 29, 61, 89–90
phallocentrism, 97, 109
plastic sexuality *see* Giddens, A.
Plummer, K., 8, 32
popular culture, 87, 94
pornography, 89, 101–102
power, 1, 4–5, 17, 23–28, 39, 40–44,
    48, 51, 53–56, 58, 61–62,
    64–65, 76–77, 87, 90–92,
    95–98, 101, 105, 121, 129, 133,
    140, 146, 149
private sphere, 16, 113
promiscuity, 43, 98–99, 100,
    104–109, 150
pure relationship *see* Giddens, A.

qualitative research methods, 1, 18,
    32, 76, 149, 152–153

reflexivity, 1, 3, 7, 10–14, 17–18,
    49, 54, 92, 94, 109, 131–133,
    142–146, 149–150
relationship breakdown, 37, 104,
    151–152
respect, 3, 8, 39–40, 44, 63, 93, 100,
    106–108, 135
retirement, 82, 84, 145–146
Richardson, D., 21–22, 103
risk, 6, 8, 13–14, 56–57, 131, 133,
    135

Robinson, V., 23, 30, 93, 98, 104, 119
romance, 9, 16, 45, 48, 52, 113, 121, 123, 126, 130
romantic love, 2–3, 5, 16, 49, 92, 125, 127–128, 142

sacrifice, 59, 61, 125, 135, 150
sampling, 30, 32
Segal, L., 24, 26–27, 88–90, 105
self-development, 4–5, 19, 131, 133–134, 136
self-help, 3, 7, 14–17, 112, 129, 133
sex
   desire, 15, 22, 28, 88, 92, 97,
   drive, 95–97, 104, 151
   frequency, 94–97
   importance of, 93–97
sexual double standard, 99
sexuality
   female, 88–89, 103, 107
   male, 27–28, 102–103
shame, 109
sixties (1960s), 1, 4–5, 9, 32, 88–89, 91, 99, 105–108, 146, 150
Smart, C., 1, 21–24, 38, 48, 53, 90, 105, 109, 133, 138, 141
social class, 19, 25, 28, 30–31, 37, 68, 90, 130, 140–141, 146, 150, 153
status, 6, 22–23, 26, 28, 40, 51, 53, 58, 60–62, 64, 74, 90, 112, 132, 134, 140, 146

taste, 37, 132, 137, 139–140, 146
ties, 2–3, 6, 10, 38, 45, 52–53, 111, 113, 149
trust, 3, 8, 103, 120

unemployment, 58
unpaid labour, 19, 24, 65, 72, 82, 85
understanding, 25–26, 30, 33, 35, 39, 42, 63, 82, 87, 91–92, 104, 109, 111, 114, 120, 122–123, 126, 127, 135–136, 142, 144, 150–151

values, 9, 12, 15, 19, 21, 30, 33, 131, 152
Victorians, 40
violence, 5, 9, 11, 89
Vogler, C., 57, 130, 150

weddings, 44, 48, 138
Weeks, J., 7, 8, 38, 48, 88, 102
work
   and gender 18, 55, 59, 61–65, 67–69, 74–75, 81–83
   hours worked 58, 60, 72, 74–75, 77,
   and identity 51, 65, 82, 146

youth, 31, 48, 52, 87, 93, 108, 142–146